Humility and Agility
The Life of a Hotelier

Humility and Agility
The Life of a Hotelier

K.B. KACHRU

ALLIED PUBLISHERS PVT. LTD.
Noida • Mumbai • Kolkata • Chennai • Bangalore

ALLIED PUBLISHERS PRIVATE LIMITED

D-5, Sector-2, **Noida**–201 301
Ph. Nos.: 0120-4320295/2542557/4352866
E-mail: delhi.books@alliedpublishers.com

17 Chittaranjan Avenue, **Kolkata**–700072
Ph.: 033-22129618 • E-mail: cal.books@alliedpublishers.com

15 J.N. Heredia Marg, Ballard Estate, **Mumbai**–400001
Ph.: 022-42126969 • E-mail: mumbai.books@alliedpublishers.com

No. 25/10, Commander-in-Chief Road, Ethiraj Lane (Next to Post Office)
Egmore, **Chennai**–600008
Ph.: 044-28223938 • E-mail: chennai.books@alliedpublishers.com

P.B. No. 9932, No. 15, 3rd Floor (Next to Vijaya Bank), 5th Cross, Gandhinagar, Karnataka, **Bangalore**–560009. Ph.: 080-41530285 / 22386239
E-mail: bngl.journals@alliedpublishers.com / apsabng@airtelmail.in

Website: www.alliedpublishers.com

ISBN: 978-93-90951-58-1

Edited by: Ms. Dipti Anand Nakai

Published by Sunil Sachdev and printed by Ravi Sachdev
at Allied Publishers Pvt. Ltd., D-5, Sector-2, Noida–201 301

Support for the Book

The success story of tourism and hospitality in India would be incomplete without the unparalleled contribution of Mr K.B. Kachru, Chairman Emeritus & Principal Advisor, Radisson Hotels Group, South Asia. He is a hotelier par excellence and his memoir is a superb handbook for all those who aspire to build memorable experiences for their customers. He has set the bar high with a stellar professional record, across the public and private sectors and has played a key role in establishing ITDC as a premier tourism and hospitality arm of the Government of India.

Amitabh Kant, *IAS*
G20 Sherpa
Ex-Chief Executive Officer
National Institute of Transforming India (NITI Aayog)

K.B. Kachru can justifiably be regarded as one of the icons of the hospitality industry and it is most gratifying that he has brought out his memoirs. He has learnt the hard way, set standards and achieved them without compromising on principles. I have had the good fortune of having him as one of my lieutenants when I headed ITDC. I had been observing his approach to work, his meticulous attention to detail, his excellent public relations, and his being able to show results out of the ordinary in the different assignments that he held. Facing stiff competition from the private sector it was no ordinary achievement to have earned the respect of the industry. ITDC acquired an enviable reputation and I basked in its glory as chairman.

Moving from the public sector to the private sector with the ease of a recognized professional was another feather in his cap.

I recommend this book to all new entrants to the industry and also to those already in it. They will profit immensely by his example.

S.K. Misra, *IAS*
Former Secretary Tourism Government of India and
Former Principal Secretary to the Prime Minister of India

During the course of his long, eventful and star-studded career, K.B. Kachru has accumulated so much experience and insight that his thoughts and memoirs will inspire succeeding generations. K.B. has had a dream run in his career. I can't recall any other person in the hospitality sector who has done so well and reached the summit of success both in the public and private sectors. This has been possible because of his integrity, single minded devotion, hard work and sagacity.

K.B.'s vision, devotion and active problem-solving attitude are commendable. He is a perfect example of a leader who leads from the front. In 1983, when I was Director General Tourism, (Government of India) the main gas tank of Ashok Hotel caught fire which could have led to an unimaginable disaster for the hotel, its occupants and employees. Not worrying about his own safety, K.B. personally led a small team and doused the fire, which helped to save many lives.

K.B. has become a legend in his lifetime. I am confident his memoirs written so truthfully and lucidly will inspire people associated with hospitality industry for long time to come.

B.K. Goswami, *IAS*
Ex-Director General (Tourism) and
Secretary, Government of India

I have known Mr. Kachru for almost 4 decades now and what a personality, what a human being, and what a professional!

A man who became youngest ever general manager of the legendary Ashok. Heading the hotel division of ITDC in his early 30's, a man responsible for bringing an international brand to India and establishing its brands in India and Indian subcontinent, as if those brands were made in India. Getting those brands present in secondary, tertiary, second tier, third tier markets whatever we want to say and last but not least, a man with all the possible Qs – his IQ, his EQ, his LQ, his PQ and his SQ. We all know IQ – the intelligence quotient, the EQ – the emotional quotient, but his LQ and PQ are probably the highest in our sector today and that is likability quotient and passion quotient. I have had the honor and privilege to get to know him closely, especially in spiritual quotient. The mention in the book about his thinking about elders, his thinking about his community, his desire and ability to contribute to the governance of the charitable and religious trusts like United Way and Vaishno Devi Trust is an inspiration. His ability to balance and adapt to the working of Public and Private sector is admirable for generations to follow.

Puneet Chhatwal
Managing Director and Chief Executive Officer
The Indian Hotels Company Ltd. (IHCL)
The Taj Group of Hotels

Many of us have watched with admiration the incredible work K.B. Kachru has done in growing and developing the brand Radisson across India and South Asia. More importantly for me, it is these great relationships and friendships that K.B. has formed along the way, which will last forever. I speak to many of the folks in the industry who speak so highly of K.B., more as a person before a professional. The experiences that he has shared in his book will be admired for many years.

Rajeev Menon
President
Marriott International Inc.
Asia Pacific excluding Greater China

Mr Kachru has been my mentor, guide, philosopher, friend, and a partner over the last seven years of my journey at the Radisson Hotel Group. His book is full of deep insights and practical wisdom. His memoirs will bring across some superbly interesting information, which is not common place, and very meaningful advice. A must read for all Hoteliers and the future leaders of tomorrow.

Zubin Saxena
Managing Director
Radisson Hotel Group, South Asia

Introduction

I landed on a cold morning in Minnesota on 9 January 2017. I had just finished what everybody in the industry considered a successful transformation of the Spanish company NH Hotel Group, and I was moving on to a possibly even more complex project as Global President of what would later be the Radisson Hotel Group. The mission was to prepare a plan that would define what to do with the two, at that moment, kind of independent 'cousins': Carlson Hotel Group and Rezidor Hotel Group.

Carlson was owner of a majority stake of the publicly listed company Rezidor. Rezidor owned and operated the business under a brand license in EMEA while Carlson owned and operated the business in the Americas and Asia – more than 1400 hotels worldwide. Two very different cultures and a traditional 'bad neighbor' relation. And both under tremendous business pressure.

When you start a project like this, as a leader your brain is focused on two major things all the time.

The first focus is to define the key elements that need to be changed, the key issues that need to be solved and define the solutions as quickly as possible.

The second is to find the people inside the company who will help you lead the change. And obviously if not, quickly try to find them outside. In my case, I look for people who believe everything is possible, who believe we are responsible for the results we have, who believe the opportunities are immense, and who fight complacency and beyond. I look for people on the inside who have the ability to change and adapt.

I met K.B. for the first time in Minneapolis at the company's headquarters, and he created a first great impression. He was listening with patience. He was explaining the areas that he thought we would have to improve to make things better. He had clarity in his mind, respect in his tone. He was talking positively about solutions and very importantly, he was candid about people. But first impressions are not enough to drive change so I visited our offices in Singapore and India in my first month at the company.

When I look for critical skills in leaders, I think there are two that are game changers when you try to drive change. Generosity and serving stakeholders. They are rare.

Generosity is not to give for free. It's about looking beyond the obvious, it's about having a win-win spirit, it's promoting empathy with your customers, external stakeholders and teams. It's about helping others to do more, to listen and coach them and make sure they deliver to their best. It's all about serving people, serving their best interests. It's being motivated not by popularity but by living concern, more than a desire for personal glory.

I have to say that I was amazed by those days together. As I talked about the global situation, K.B. was reflecting on the one in South Asia. We talked about the changes needed in the organization. We talked about the vision of becoming one of the top three brands in the world for consumers, owners and employees. We shared the difficult situation in which we were. We talked about the issues and opportunities. We talked about the courage we needed from everybody to take the company to a new level. We were truly aligned. Not only in the what, but also on the how.

He embraced the method I had designed to bring the five-year-plan to life and became one of the ambassadors of change in the company. And as a great leader, he got his hands dirty, not only theoretically. He was driving the changes in the organization and executing the same. And he did it with generosity, in relationships and managing to stay aligned with the tourism industry's and government of India's growth plans.

I have taken this opportunity to reveal to you something I always felt but never shared even with K.B. The Radisson Hotel Group has successfully transformed its business and organization, and is on track to the vision we defined in 2017 after only five years. But actually, this vision had already been achieved in India under K.B.'s leadership. As a founding partner of the company, K.B. had driven the Carlson/Radisson Group to become the largest international hotel group in South Asia at that moment and accelerated it during this period to have over 160 hotels in operation and under development. But he never told me, 'Fede, you are trying to do what I already did.' I knew it. Possibly he knew it, too... But he only focused on how he would help the change and achieve even higher targets.

The book you are going to read will help you know the man and the leader K.B. is. And beyond that, I believe it will help you learn how to be happy and at the same time be successful.

His many exciting and some harrowing experiences as written in the chapter 'Flashbacks and Memorable Experiences' will give you an insight on how he was able to absorb speed bumps.

The chapter on 'Leaving the Public Sector' reflects that it is not easy for professionals in India to move from the public sector to the private sector, particularly under difficult circumstances.

K.B.'s vision and commitment to start the Carlson/RHG brands from ground zero in Asia has been well articulated in the chapter on 'Carlson Hospitality and the Radisson Hotel Group', where he talks about 'predicting your own future by creating it'.

As articulated in the chapter on 'Ideas on Leadership', there are great learnings for future leaders with an emphasis on empowerment – having a succession plan, taking a step back, the secrets of dealing with people, compassion and most importantly, relationship building.

I am glad to work with K.B. because he is a gift. He is a happy man who is successful – very successful and very happy.

I mentioned what you will read, but I want to highlight something that you will not read in the book but I hope you will imagine as you do. K.B. has 'presence'. I do not know how to define it well. When K.B. is in a meeting, you know he is there. Even if he does not speak. You happen to see that he is smarter than you, a good person, a person who cares for people, a person obsessed with doing better, a person with curiosity and initiative. This is a gift he has. And we are happy he shares it with us.

Enjoy the journey! He is enjoying his.

Federico J. González
Executive Vice-Chairman
Radisson Hotel Group and
Group Chief Executive Officer
Louvre Hotels Group

Foreword

I had the privilege of meeting K.B. Kachru in 2008 when I became the CEO of Carlson Companies, the family-owned, Minneapolis-based travel and hospitality company that owned Carlson Wagonlit Travel, Carlson Hotels (Regent, Radisson, Country Inns & Suites), Carlson Marketing, Regent Seven Seas Cruises, and TGI Fridays.

K.B. was leading Carlson Hotels' activities in South Asia. He had been an entrepreneurial pioneer for decades and played a critical role in building the business to its position of pre-eminence in the region.

I was immediately struck by K.B.'s kindness and his humility. It was clear from the outset that K.B. had been leading by developing authentic, human relationships that had been impactful and enduring.

This was obvious in his relationship with his colleagues, who he cared deeply about, to the point that he mentored many great leaders and invested deeply in their development. It is noteworthy that several of them ended up moving up to positions of significant leadership. This was also true in his relationship with colleagues from other Carlson businesses. Critically important, it was particularly true with Carlson's hotel owners and its key business partners in the region (Rajan Jetley and Ranjan Bhattacharya spring to mind).

It was not difficult for me to decide to trust K.B. and challenge him to continue to lead our growth in this strategic market and do even more.

Not surprisingly therefore, the book that K.B. has written – *Humility and Agility: The Life of a Hotelier* – reminds us the importance of several important human truths. Amongst many, there are three that stand out for me:

1. *Our life is a journey*. I love this quote that K.B. shares with us from Peter Hagerty: 'Life is a journey, and if you fall in

love with the journey, you will be in love forever.' And it is a wonderful gift that K.B. has taken the time to share key moments and lessons from his journey so far!

2. *Everything starts with people and authentically connecting with them.* This is for sure true in the hospitality sector. Throughout his career, K.B. has role modelled this beautiful behavior that every leader can embrace.
3. *Leadership has a lot to do with empowering others.* K.B. knows this from his own experience. As the sixth president of the United States John Quincy Adams reputedly said, 'If your actions inspire others to dream more, learn more, do more, and become more, you are a leader.'

From his childhood in the Kashmir Valley, to his initiation to the industry, his rise in it, and then his passing the baton to the next generation of leaders, K.B.'s beautifully written book takes us through many vivid, inspiring moments and jaw-dropping stories, from which he distills for us key leadership lessons. It is particularly fascinating to discover K.B.'s early calling to join the hospitality sector, and how he overcame his parents' concerns, and pursued his dream in such a determined and talented fashion.

Every step along the way in K.B.'s journey is portrayed vividly and compellingly and K.B.'s strong, calm, beautiful wisdom transpires in every page, in every adventure, in every human connection, in every relationship.

As a remarkable exclamation mark, K.B.'s 'Ideas on Leadership', which he distills in chapter VIII, are pure gold.

My life is better because I have gotten to know K.B. Kachru. Thank you, K.B., for touching my heart and inspiring many others.

Hubert Joly

Member of the board of directors for Johnson & Johnson and Ralph Lauren Corporation Worldwide

Former chairman and chief executive officer of Best Buy Inc., and Carlson Companies USA,

Presently teaching at Harvard Business School,

Author, The Heart of Business – Leadership Principles for the Next Era of Capitalism

Preface

In early 2021, I was at lunch with a group of seven close friends, fondly referred to as G7, in New Delhi. Being from different industries and backgrounds, we often stumble into conversations about our most pivotal experiences, the chances we didn't take, the changes we embraced that made us who we are. As I narrated an incident about why I left the hospitality trade in the public sector, they prompted me to open up to them about a host of colourful anecdotes and later suggested I consider compiling my many adventures in a book.

I was hesitant at first, not because I didn't have much to share – I do – but because I wondered whether these stories across decades in the dynamic world of hospitality would be of interest to anyone outside my family and close circle of friends. I discussed it with my wife, Neelam, and recognized that within my hesitation there was also a compulsion. Peter Hagerty's words – of Goldman Sachs fame – rang true for me: 'Life is a journey, and if you fall in love with the journey, you will be in love forever.' I discovered a motivation that was filled with gratitude and appreciation for my life as a hotelier, and from this purview, I became more confident that sharing my experiences could be an act of service for aspiring entrants, my colleagues, and of course, my near and dear ones. I consulted close friends and few industry colleagues, who strongly recommended I pursue the project. My daughter-in-law Gazzal is an avid reader of biopics, who when presented with early drafts of these essays, also encouraged me to continue writing.

This memoir is a kind of fait accompli, in the making long before I decided that it could be. At several points I was unsure whether I should go ahead, but I was inspired by the extraordinary courage others display in sharing their life stories, and especially the controversial experiences one encounters. I've tried to be as candid and forthcoming as possible. In this book, I share stories about my upbringing, why I chose hospitality as a career, my foray into leadership at a very nascent age and in general, my life's learnings. I've been fortunate to be able to reasonably chart my own journey as well as create some opportunities for future generations. Since it is difficult to encapsulate a life overall in a few words, particularly in the context of a profession I cherish so deeply, I have only chosen anecdotes in which I was directly involved, hoping to give my reader an insider's glimpse into the hospitality business through the challenges that came my way and an understanding of how I overcame them.

Hospitality to me is no less than breathing fresh air. Going the extra mile invigorates me, and an enthused mind has helped me to try, excel and value what I am today. In the last four or five decades, Indian hospitality has blossomed with changing market dynamics and I've been fortunate to have played some part in driving this change. Facilitating the entry of multinational brands in our part of the world, particularly in the mid-scale and upscale segments in emerging markets, creating new food concepts, and executing well-defined, standard operating procedures have been part of my key achievements, especially in the last twenty years. What may further interest readers is the insight I share on how Indian hospitality has moved away from socialistic thinking towards new-age comfort and luxury. The mindset of potential investors, guests' expectations and connectivity have also changed in the recent past.

I have had the advantage of working in both the public and private sectors. During my stint in the public sector, except on a few occasions, I did not face any bureaucratic or political interference, otherwise considered the norm in a government undertaking, though some of my experiences might make one think otherwise. Working with Carlson Hospitality and the Radisson Hotel Group has been most rewarding as I was able to introduce and operationalize their first hotels in Bangladesh, Indonesia, Malaysia, Thailand, Nepal, Mauritius and India. It was indeed challenging to start from ground zero in these countries and yet manage to establish the hotels as leaders in some regions. In setting up four joint ventures for Carlson, I was tasked with identifying our strategic partners, seeking majority funding and motivating them to commit to the development schedule for our expansion plans. In the year 2019, we as Carlson/RHG hotels were acknowledged as the largest international hotel company in South Asia.

My enriching interactions with the world's top dignitaries, including prime ministers, presidents and royalty, form part of my memoir. These experiences are precious to me as only a few of us have had the privilege to meet such illustrious people in life. I have given an account of my experiences with some of the most controversial persons in the world and what it was like getting to intimately observe and know them. I have also shared details of my time with the India Tourism Development Corporation (ITDC), an undertaking of the Government of India. During my tenure at ITDC and the Ashok Group of Hotels, I initiated the first-ever franchising process in the public sector and also oversaw the establishment and operation of the Moscow–Ashok Corporation in the erstwhile Soviet Union. These hard-working years were not only exciting and adventurous but also testing at times, and I have made mention of the creation of many joint ventures with reputed investors, national and international companies as well as state governments.

The book also outlines my personal journey in the trade and mentions my family, my memories from travel and friendships made over the years, which I consider among my lifetime achievements. I feel blessed to have received the same affection and respect from people who worked for and with me even forty years ago, and share the mentoring I've given to and received from many successful individuals who have achieved high positions in the industry.

Since hospitality attracts a lot of media attention, I am grateful for the positive attention and many awards and accolades I have received throughout my career from the government, as well as international and domestic travel-and-tourism industry platforms. I am honoured to have been nominated on the boards of various government and semi-government undertakings, besides serving on the boards of various national and international charitable trusts and organizations.

Most importantly, I wish to stress on the truth of experience. The hospitality business may look easy and glamourous on the outside, but behind the magic show is a grueling and challenging life. To succeed in this trade, one must be prepared to commit to hard work, initiative and humility. In all honesty, I also touch upon how important it is to be lucky, to be at the right place at the right time…

Acknowledgements

I deeply appreciate and acknowledge the opportunity to be part of both the India Tourism Development Corporation and Radisson Hotels Group, which have presented me with a platform in the hospitality and tourism industry in India and South Asia for over four decades.

While writing the book I was inspired by my social interactions, it was my wife Neelam who encouraged me to document my life's journey, career and thoughts. Neelam is the centre of my life. She has not only inspired me to reach great heights but also has always been a paragon of support. She approached writing this manuscript whole-heartedly, and it is only with her help, dedication and agile remembrances – as she had been privy to most things – that we were able to complete this project together.

A very special thanks to Dipti Anand Nakai for agreeing to edit my book. Over a period of time, she patiently read through and edited numerous versions of the manuscript. She supplied detailed comments and questions, and constructive advice, which gave the manuscript a final shape and structure.

I greatly appreciate the inputs of Mr Ravindra Kumar, managing director and editor-in-chief of the *Statesman*, who read an early version of the manuscript and advised me on how to make the book more meaningful, readable and relevant.

A big thank you to Allied Publishers and its team – especially to Ravi Sachdev and Sunil Sachdev, dear friends whom I have known since the eighties – for putting their faith in me and publishing this book. I am grateful to Sharad Gupta for all the coordination.

I would like to thank Mr Federico González and Mr Hubert Joly for writing the introduction and foreword. Many thanks to

Mr Amitabh Kant, Mr S.K. Misra, Mr B.K. Goswami, Mr Puneet Chhatwal, Mr Rajeev Menon, Mr Nitin Kapur and Mr Zubin Saxena for their early consideration and support for this book. Gratitude to other mentors and industry colleagues for writing their generous endorsements and kind words.

Kalpana Negi for her involvement in collating information and helping me to retrieve an archive of old documents and photographs, etc.

I am grateful for God's blessings and the love I receive from my family and friends, which has motivated me to keep humble and agile.

Contents

I

Childhood, Family and Kashmir

The sun first rises on the golden years

Decades ago, I was on a holiday in Delhi, visiting my sister. It was a hot and blustery morning, and I was pressed against the window seat of a rickety DTC bus, the stifling air doing nothing to cool my dampened shirt collar. I was mostly daydreaming, but something in the fugue caught my attention. It was a street hoarding that called out: 'Study Hotel Management at Pusa Road'. I felt a marvellous flutter travel through me, which made me sit up straighter and take note of the thoughts quickly forming in my head. Suddenly, I knew – this is what I may want.

As serendipitous as my sparking interest in the hospitality industry was, the truth is that I was looking for a way out. As with most Indian families, my parents wanted me to be a doctor, engineer or civil servant, and in my case they levied emphasis on healthcare. I felt a relatable, mounting pressure to succumb in my school years, and to make matters worse, most of my peers and almost all my cousins were studying to become either engineers or doctors. Young Indians today have more liberties and are perhaps better placed and prepared to choose their own careers, including in the hospitality and travel sectors that are considered not only viable but lucrative options. But back in 1968, when I had just graduated from school and was planning out my future, this was not the case. Where persuasion did not work, I considered outright rebellion. To become a doctor was nowhere on my agenda and I needed to somehow convince my parents that I was not cut out to be one.

A few days after I had seen the advertisement for the Institute of Hotel Management (IHM), Pusa Road, I decided to visit the college. I took a bus to the address I'd noted only to discover a mom-and-pop operation that taught French and a few other basic courses that could lead to small-time jobs in hotels. I was dismayed and slouched out of one of the rooms with a heavy heart, already dreading medical school. Just then I came across another desk tucked away in the corner of the building, manned by a busy-looking gentleman. I asked him if that was all there was to the massive advertisement I had seen, and he shook his head. 'No, no, no… this isn't the institute,' he said. 'Come, I'll give you directions.' My spirits rose again. I followed the route he indicated and walked a while under the hot sun until the huge gates of the Pusa Institute glimmered their welcome. The shady tree-lined driveway offered a breath of cool air and the hope of a future. But once again, I was at a loss. The institute seemed primarily focused on agricultural research; I couldn't see any sign of a hotel management school. Perhaps it was my deep-seated desire to make something of myself out of my own choice that something urged me not to give up. What I would have given for a quick Google Maps search back then! After many inquiries, I finally stumbled upon a brand-new, extensively constructed building surrounded by manicured lawns. The moustachioed guard at the entrance gave me a welcoming smile and directed me to the administrator's office. Once inside, I met the very pleasant Mr R.A. Gupta, manager of administration, who sold me a prospectus that contained the application form. He told me the deadline was fast approaching and that I should apply as soon as possible. I headed straight home to show the prospectus to my brother-in-law, the late C.N. Kaul, a chartered accountant working at the World Health Organization, who saw worth in my dream. After some conversations back-and-forth, he accompanied me to the college. To my good fortune, Mr Gupta turned out to be my brother-in-law's batch-mate and after their meeting, he was quick to give me his approval.

When my brother-in-law broke the news of my decision to my parents, they were in uproar. 'Are you going to make our son a cook or waiter?' my mother exclaimed. But he argued that dynamics had changed and it was no longer the case that only doctors and engineers made a good living; other careers also offered good opportunities. He added that I would only excel in a profession that I loved. It was easier for us to convince my father, who was well educated and had a broader vision than my mother, even though he would have also preferred I become a doctor because it was more conventional, and in their eyes, more stable. But he soon agreed. Over fifty years ago, the perspective of the women in my family was limited, and my mother had very little or perhaps no exposure to this industry and the glamour and prestige connected with it. Hospitality runs in Kashmiri blood I told her, and argued that I am a thoroughbred Kashmiri. In those days the people of the Kashmir Valley boasted of a cultural hospitality that was perhaps the rarest in the world. We were known to be very caring, effusive at welcoming guests whom we not only fed well but over-fed, sometimes even to a point of irritation. I continued to look for support elsewhere but my friends in Jammu also said to me: 'You don't need to go to college to be a caterer or *tawaza* officer. God help you and your family!' For a while after, I had to put up with their lectures on how I was going to ruin my life if I persisted with this mad-cap idea. My mother went a step further and did not speak to me for six months. Amidst taunts to my mother from our extended family of how her son was going to become a glorified cook or waiter, it was my brother-in-law who finally convinced her to allow me to pursue an education in hotel management. Meanwhile, to assuage everyone, I enrolled myself in a pre-med programme at the science college to bring about some peace at home.

Admission at IHM Pusa, even back in the day, was competitive. Hundreds of students applied to secure a spot among a meagre sixty seats. My parents lived in Jammu & Kashmir but I especially returned to Delhi to hand-deliver my application before the deadline. I had an interview afterwards, but I wasn't sure how it went since one of the interviewers unexpectedly asked me how to make tomato sauce. My reply was, 'I don't know how. I will know if I am admitted to the course.' Imagine my joy when I was selected. As one of the first few students from the state of Jammu & Kashmir to join a formal programme in hospitality, my excitement grew further when I received a scholarship from the government, likely the first in the state, as support for venturing into the profession. The financial aid was helpful to me and my parents. Tourism has historically been one of the biggest contributors to the state's gross development product. Being in government service and in the media, my father was aware that it was possible to obtain a scholarship for students from the state pursuing this industry. He guided me on how to go about applying for it.

In a matter of a few months, I was packing my bags to leave my beautiful hometown, the place I was born in, to study in the capital city. Kashmir is not only picturesque and enchanting but also laid-back. Srinagar is a lush green valley cradled in the Himalayas, surrounded by mountain peaks and glistening lakes. I was leaving behind this beautiful land where I had so many childhood memories of picnicking in the famous Mughal gardens, sitting on the green grass drinking *sheer* chai (salted pink tea) straight from the Samovar, which was kept hot by lighted coal. I wondered how I would fit into the new cosmopolitan life that awaited me. I had once visited the then Oberoi Palace Hotel (now the Lalit) in Srinagar and seen many Bollywood celebrities hanging around the hotel. The hotel is an actual palace converted into a five-star property with sprawling lawns overlooking the magnificent Dal Lake. This was my first vivid impression of the kind of hotels I wanted to be associated with, and I was thrilled at the prospects of eventually working at one.

As a young boy from a small town, I must admit that I was attracted to the glamour and luxury the industry has to offer. I expected that my job could take me to remote and exotic locations and that I would get to meet the who's-who of the world. Of course I was nervous, but I was also excited. Even as my parents had been forced to believe in me, I was determined to believe in myself. I was not going to let them down. I had placed my bets on the Institute of Hotel Management, Catering & Nutrition, as it was called back then, and I had every intention of succeeding even as my mother still harboured the hope that I would change my mind and come home to become a doctor.

My father, the late Somnath Kachru, was the youngest of three siblings. Both his sister and brother were gentle people and not as educated as my father, who had an undergraduate college degree, which was considered a big deal in those days. My grandfather died when my father was only a few years old. The family lived in a joint ancestral house in Rainawari, Srinagar, where my grandmother brought up her children with the help of the extended family. My father, who was known as 'Papaji' to all, including my sister and me, also lived for many years in Mr Balkak Dhar's house, a relative of my grandmother's. There he shared a room with Mr D.P. Dhar, who later became ambassador to Russia in the seventies and thereafter a senior Cabinet Minister in the Central Government. This was my grandmother's way of ensuring that Papaji received a good education and also grew up with strong values and vision. He and my mother Gauri Kaul Gassi, one of the most beautiful girls of her time, were married when my mother was in her early teens. Her father was a senior customs officer, and she too had been brought up in a big joint family. Soon after their wedding, my father left for Kanpur for further studies. My mother continued to live with her parents till he completed his education.

My sister Raj is almost ten years older than me. As a late-comer into the family, I hear that my mother and her parents went from doctors to saints in pursuit of her to conceive again. When I was eight-years-old, my father was transferred from Srinagar and we had to relocate to Jammu, where I was admitted to Model Academy School and eventually graduated from there. As a young boy, I was obedient, quiet and respectful; the kind of child that parents are proud of. Although I was an average student, school teachers never complained about me. I can still vividly recall my participation in annual celebrations, or National Cadet Corps (NCC) classes, though my excitement to be a cadet was limited to the free *samosas* and *mithai* they gave us to snack. I do regret that I couldn't remain in Srinagar and finish high school at CMS Tyndale–Biscoe School. When I was fourteen-years-old, my father was posted in Jalandhar as assistant director of All India Radio Jalandhar. I also moved with my parents and took admission at DAV School, which I barely attended for a month. The atmosphere of the school was too different from what I was used to, so I persuaded my parents to allow me to return to Jammu. Back in Jammu, I lived alone in half of the house; the other half had been rented to a South Indian army officer. He and his wife soon became very fond of me so food was not an issue, and overall I was happy to be back in my hometown. Perhaps it was simply adolescence or the lack of parental supervision, but for a while in-between I became rambunctious, keeping not such great company and suddenly getting into trouble more often than not. Luckily my parents lived in the bliss of ignorance, and I never got around to telling them about this. One time a group of rival boys threw me into the canal but I managed to hold onto some large wild reeds and weeds for dear life.

The Kashmiri Pandit community in the 1960s consisted largely of bureaucrats and was a middle-class society. Most families earned enough to meet their basic needs. Food was the major expense, yet every household's focus was on the variety of mutton dishes they could serve to guests. Homes were very simple, with almost all of them fitted with a *takhtposh* (wooden settee) used for sitting, eating and in some cases sleeping too. Ours was one of the few homes that had a drawing room with a sofa set. My father was a forward-looking person and tried to create reforms within a ritualistic Kashmiri Pandit society, especially regarding the expenses involved at the time of death in the family. In the eighties, he even contested for a position in the Kashmiri Pandit Sabha in Jammu but lost, as most people were too orthodox and unprepared for change. His opponents were able to influence voters' thoughts by saying that my father was trying to put an end to our traditions and culture.

My mother was worldly wise and nothing gave her more pleasure than feeding, or rather over-feeding, relatives and friends. She barely had any time left from cooking and socializing, but my father was always there for me. He would spend quality time with me in the evenings after work, helping me do my homework and playing with me, while teaching me how to be a good person. When we lived in Srinagar, he would take me for weekly outings to Ahdoo's for pastries, *kanti* kababs and *kahwa*. Later, even my children were very fond of him, often making him into a horse and riding on his back, and he was always happy to do whatever pleased them. My father was a house-proud person and stood apart from his peers in characteristic ways. He spoke eloquent English with a cosmopolitan lilt, unlike the accent so typical of the Valley. He had a keen sense of humour, which unfortunately bypassed me, but both my sons inherited it. After retiring from All India Radio, he wrote articles on various topics for the *Kashmir Times*. He was immaculately dressed, mostly in well-fitted suits with shoes that were always polished to a mirror finish. I am fortunate to have inherited the best from both my mother and father, who among other things, shared great influence in shaping my interpersonal skills.

For the better part of my life, my older sister Raj was almost like another mother to me. She was married to Chand Narain Kaul when I was only ten-years-old. My brother-in-law, who worked most of his life at WHO, retired at sixty as the chief of finance at their worldwide headquarters in Geneva. He was also an accomplished golfer and had a wonderful sense of humour, and he guided me well and whole-heartedly through my formative years. While at IHM Pusa, I visited their home as often as I could get away from the hostel. I was made to feel welcome in their house in South Extension, where they lived with his parents. One day, as a gesture of gratitude, I decided to take my sister's ageing father- and mother-in-law to watch a movie, which I had very carefully selected believing it would be religious and hence most appropriate for people their age. The film was *Dharmatma*, and to my chagrin the film turned out to be anything but pious. It is, in fact, the Hindi version of the Hollywood film the *Godfather*. I cannot express the embarrassment I faced at the explicit violence and sex, sitting wedged between them in the cinema hall. But I recovered quickly from the incident.

When I left home to study in New Delhi, my father had said to me: 'I trust in you. Don't breach this faith. I say this since you will be your own master going forward.' He was a wise man. In saying these words, he made me responsible for myself in life. I promised myself that I would never do anything that may hurt him because I loved him so dearly. His happiness and validation meant everything to me. I felt I needed to become someone who would 'make a difference' to this world, not only because that's what I wanted to do, but also to prove to myself and my parents that I had chosen the right path.

To briefly jump ahead in time, I had never imagined that I would find my life partner at IHM Pusa, and that too someone who was not from my community. I believe it was destiny that made us both meet and take the decision to spend our lives together. Once I joined Pusa, I realized I needed to be especially mindful when choosing a life partner. She would have to be someone who would understand and empathize with the life of a hotelier, who would not complain if I came home late every evening, which is so typical of a hotelier's life.

I was engaged to Neelam on 25 November 1973 at the principal of the Pusa Institute's home lawns, as defining moment in my life as any. It was such that as soon as we exchanged rings my destiny announced itself again. Within minutes, my training manager Psyche Nigam informed me that the interviews for the Carl Duisburg Gesellschaft Scholarships for Germany were taking place the next morning, and since I was already in Delhi I should appear for them. The interview went well and I was selected. This scholarship was the first of many incredible opportunities to come my way.

We were just twenty-two-years-old when we married with full tradition and fanfare. Despite great resistance from our parents, who believed that we were mismatched, our wedding was a grand affair despite my meagre resources. I was able to borrow the Maharaja Hari Singh's Achkan (a long coat made with gold thread) which he had worn for his own wedding. Maharaja Hari Singh was the last king of Jammu & Kashmir. The Achkan is now an exhibit in the museum in Jammu. Neelam and I have been married for almost half-a-century and even after all these years of togetherness, in which challenges and adventures have both abounded, it seems the years have simply flown by. I am fortunate to have found in her a partner in all respects. Neelam has worked beside me for many years and simultaneously excelled at enriching our home and personal lives. There have been times that I have guided her on what to do and other times I have also taken her advice very seriously. I know that if there is anyone who can and will be frank with me, it is her, sometimes to the point of even upsetting me. Still, she is the only one I know who will be truthful to a fault and never misguide me.

Naturally we have often had our differences, which mostly emanate from our distinct cultural backgrounds. I come from a humble and orthodox Kashmiri family, and she was born to a Sindhi father and a Punjabi mother. Being from two communities, Neelam has always expressed herself as broader minded. Her father, Mr Ram Panjwani, was a successful businessman and highly respected by all who knew him. He was very well connected and had contacts all over the world, which included prominent business leaders in India, some of whom I had the good fortune of meeting through him early in my career. My father-in-law was a visionary and a great philanthropist for the poor and orphaned. He was a strict father to Neelam but even sixty years ago, he had the instinct to send his only daughter to study at Welham Girls' School in Dehradun, one of the most reputed boarding schools in the country, which is where Neelam virtually grew up. I am told that her grandfather did not approve of the expenses involved in this education, so her father set up an independent insurance business to pay for her schooling. She was born in the holy city of Haridwar, where the family had moved after the Partition. Back in those early post-Independence days, when few girls barely studied till class ten, he had the foresight to ensure that his daughter receives the best education. While in school he encouraged her to pursue all extracurricular activities. She was a good hockey player and not only played for her school team but was also selected to play at the state level. Neelam has also had a knack for languages and embodies an artistic bent of mind. Once she graduated from Welham's, Neelam joined IHM Pusa in Delhi to study hotel management in the hope of equipping herself with an education in management and home economic skills that would help her support her future family as needed. This is where we met; how we met is a story I'll wait to share shortly.

Neelam and I have been blessed with two sons – Amit and Sameer. Our older son Amit lives in Minneapolis, USA, along with his wife Bhavna and their teenage daughter Anya. Our younger son Sameer lives with us in New Delhi, with his wife Gazzal, son Aahil and daughter Ashyra. We love our sprawling family and look forward to spending quality time with all of them either on weekends in Delhi, annual holidays to America, or frequent family vacations in Europe. When our children were growing up, we were too busy at work and did not have the pleasure of enjoying their childhood. Today our grandchildren add years to lives, coaxing second childhoods out of us.

My mother, whom I lost recently at the age of ninety-four, also lived with us ever since my father passed away in 1986. My father was my first mentor; he remained my guide for as long as he lived and was like a friend to me. He told Neelam soon after our wedding: 'I feel very proud that now people call me Bhushanji's father instead of him being known as my son.' I am grateful to have felt his pride in me during his lifetime, even as the mysterious ways of the Almighty took him away from us too early. He suffered from liver cancer, albeit never having tasted liquor. There was no cure available for liver cancer in the country in the eighties, and he went away within just three months. Neelam dedicated herself to him during that time, personally cooking each meal for him and also feeding him his food and medicines till the end.

I have remembered and missed my father most at every milestone I achieved in my career. Together Neelam and I have built a professional and personal life that we are both proud of. Working together with Neelam has never been an issue for us, both in the government job at ITDC and at the Carlson Hospitality Group. Though I do not believe our situation is unique in the business world, since plenty of couples work alongside each other, I do feel thankful to have her be a person in whom I have complete faith. I commend her for her devotion to the job and her capabilities and strengths. Neelam has also looked after the family to the best of her abilities, and I've always respected her for giving up furthering her career to bring up and take care of the children. She is the anchor of my life and family.

II

Initiation to the Industry

No ability without opportunity,
and a few strokes of luck

My years at the Pusa Institute in Delhi were filled with long hours, and our curriculum was structured in such a manner that we learned to 'dirty our hands' in all aspects of the industry. I must admit I was not too keen on quantity kitchen training – most of it was to prepare food for hostellers and the housekeeping jobs involved only regular cleaning. My interests were always focused on more creative and definite learnings, even if that meant the cleaning of stains from different surfaces like hard-stone, fabrics, furniture, etc. But I enjoyed our college bakery classes that were run by Papa Mendonca, as we fondly called him. We could also buy these fancy and delicious baked goods at a nominal cost, and we would take our haul along with us when visiting relatives who were more than happy to receive them, as such quality products were unavailable in shops those days.

I was happy to learn and coast along my college years, which felt as carefree as they were inspiring. Then, in my third year, during our college elections to select class representatives, a desire to assume a leadership role overtook me. I didn't aggressively opt to get into this role but I experienced a palpable change of mindset when I felt compelled to do things for the good of the institute and its students. So I contested the election and won. I ended up becoming the president of the student association, merely by chance, because the person we had all been supporting backed out at the last minute. The hostlers decided they would only back a guy from the hostel. Although I was contented with where I was, the timing was equally relevant in the opportunity being provided to me, and for a chance to be successful, I feel a confident self-positioning is absolutely important. At this stage, a fourth-year student named Neelam Panjwani was nominated by the then principal Mr J.P. Sharma to the Student Association Board. He said it was in line with the Constitution and he was well within his rights to nominate one outstanding student, but it was also the first time a principal had exercised the right to do so. My peers and I were not happy about his decision because we believed Neelam would be like a watch-dog over us. So I, along with other members and hostellers, approached her to resign. Since she didn't even know of the principal's decision, she outrightly refused saying that she could not resign from a nomination as she was not an elected candidate. Thus began my first fling at leadership, with some opposition planted by none other than the head of the institution. Little did I know at the time that I had also found my life partner.

Mr J.P. Sharma was a dynamic principal, an accomplished hotelier and a graduate of Blackpool Hotel School. He strived to position IHM Pusa as a leading hotel management institution, even while Mumbai Catering College was the market leader at that time. It was with Mr Sharma's guidance that the student association's funds were used towards the development of students and their futures. We organized business interactions and talent and product presentations to media and industry leaders, and also ensured that campus recruitments by almost all hotel chains were undertaken for the very first time. No hospitality companies had conducted campus recruitments until then. We participated in industry competitions, which further enhanced the visibility of our institution, and in turn helped most of us get management trainee positions. I remember an instance when the government and Delhi Tourism Board organized an all-India cooking competition at the Red Fort. There was a lot of media hype around it and the news was covered all over the country. Neelam and I, as a team, got the opportunity to participate and won the first prize. I was most excited by workshops that focused on the delivery of nutritious food at all pricing levels. In the sixties and seventies, there was hardly any consciousness around health food but certain agencies offered IHM students opportunities to create tasty and healthy food recipes. Similarly, several architectural firms held design contests where we were given the opportunity to participate.

I still fondly recall the educational tour we organized, and therefore feel it is worth a mention. We decided to give real-time exposure to students and visit tourist destinations around India, and essentially included hotels and industrial catering institutions as part of our itinerary. We travelled extensively, including places like Sanchi, Gwalior, Hyderabad, Mumbai and of course, the famous Khajuraho temples. Overall the trip was great fun as well as educational. The Khajuraho temples opened our eyes to a part of our culture and heritage that was previously beyond our imagination. The girls went to see the temples separately because they were too shy to stand around the erotic statues with the boys. Sanchi was also a special visit; one evening, we built a huge bonfire on a hilltop to ward off the cold December breeze and sang and danced around it till early in the morning. Our train was delayed by hours, and we even slept on the railway platform till it arrived – an experience I can never forget. A funny incident occurred on the day we were to make the train bookings. Our critic Neelam (now my wife) decided that we must not be allowed to travel by taxis and should only use DTC buses. She herself had never been seen boarding a bus so we challenged her to come along with us. She had no choice but to agree, however in the end she didn't turn up, later claiming it was because her father had been visiting from Haridwar. Her inability to join us worked in our favour and somehow became a turning point; from then on she stopped opposing us for the sake of it and we started working as a team going forward. It is on this very same educational tour in Mumbai that Neelam and I realized that we had grown attached to each other. Her father had organized a car at each destination to be at her disposal. The rest of us had booked a coach to take us around. One day, as we were separated by transport and logistics, we were both uncomfortable and knew instantly that we missed each other. Without knowing what the future had in store for us, a relationship of the hearts was gradually taking shape. It was also on this trip to Mumbai that I had my first lesson in eating with chopsticks. Chinese cuisine was Neelam's favourite, and I had yet to develop a taste for this exotic cuisine, which was still becoming popular in India. Our classmate and friend Ng Seng Yong, a Singaporean citizen, told me that I must develop a taste for Chinese food in order to be Neelam's friend and told her that she must start watching Hindi movies with interest. Neelam had grown up in a British atmosphere, watching only English films at Welham's.

Once back in Delhi, we both decided that the college must have a monthly newsletter out of a desire to communicate the good work we were doing, the response we were receiving from the industry as a whole as well as furthering opportunities for students. Of course, I can't deny that it was certainly a good excuse to be together. Neelam would collect all the material, write and edit the magazine, and we would both then walk down to the printer's shop in East Patel Nagar. We needed to take numerous trips to the printer, and this became our evening ritual. Sometimes we took the time out to go for coffee or watch a movie together. I was only eighteen-years-old and even at this young age, I was done with my share of crushes and knew that I had found the person who would be a perfect life partner for me. I decided to seal the relationship as soon as possible, and one sunny morning before going into our respective lecture rooms, I stopped her outside the college building. To her surprise, I asked her to marry me. To my delight she said, 'Yes'. Happily, we both proceeded to attend our respective lectures.

Our final examinations took place in the middle of summer. I did try to submit my projects and journals on time, for which I took help from my batchmates, but to my bad luck I developed a severe allergy in the weeks leading up to my deadlines. My eyes were swollen and I could not read. We didn't really study from textbooks for most subjects, just cyclostyled handouts and mostly our own notes from class lectures. But Neelam came to my rescue even though she had to prepare for her own examinations. She helped me prepare my notes and even read them out to me since my vision was blurred. Thankfully I passed with a good result in all subjects and she topped her class too, which saved me from any guilt.

During the course of my three years at the Pusa Institute, each of us had to complete 'on-the-job' training during our summer vacations. After my first year, I completed some training in Srinagar because I still had dreams of becoming a *tawaza* (catering) officer in the Jammu & Kashmir Department of Tourism after completing the programme. That summer was one of my most memorable sojourns in my homeland. I worked at Kolahoi, a restaurant at Broadway Theatre. I lived with my grandparents who pampered me with homemade Kashmiri food, whenever I got to eat with them. I otherwise ate staff meals at the restaurant. What I reminisce and narrate to others with humour is the number of bread slices that I could and would eat at the restaurant. The staff was prohibited from eating butter, so I would consume up to a bottle of tomato ketchup with a loaf of bread in a single meal.

After my second year, I completed some training at the Oberoi Clarkes Hotel in Shimla. Students played a small role, if any, in selecting where they were to be trained; the faculty arranged and decided our training placements for us. But a providential me went yet again to another hill resort in the summer. The Oberoi Clarkes Shimla was the first property owned by the Oberoi family. It was a small property with a modest inventory of rooms, but at that time the who's-who of India came to vacation there during the summer. The property was built by the British in 1898 and retained its colonial beginnings and splendour. Mr Panna Lal, the general manager, was a fine gentleman. Three of us from IHM Pusa had been sent there, and in those good old days the Oberois were generous to assign us a room at the hotel, that too next to Mrs M.S. Oberoi herself. Being next door to her proved to be of great advantage to us. She often inquired whether our training was going well and if we required anything. She would pray regularly and offer us *prasad* afterwards. The flip side of this generosity was that we had to maintain discipline at all times, making no noise and not attracting any attention that could affect our stay at the hotel. That I could stay at the hotel and eat in the staff dining room excited me to no end. It was my first experience with luxury and I loved every minute of it. I also had umpteen opportunities to interact with Rai Bahadur M.S. Oberoi, who visited the hotel often. Though I trained at the front office, my training was far beyond just learning the technical aspects of running small hotels; I learned so much about dealing with people. The fun bit was that I got to know each guest personally, most of whom were from affluent families and travelled in large groups, as well as many Bollywood stars who would dance to the band every night till the wee hours of the morning. Others were honeymooners, who were often very formal with each other on arrival as most of them would have had arranged marriages, and I was privy to seeing how their romance grew each day till they returned home. There were other times when couples would fight and I would find myself sympathizing with one of the spouses or even playing the role of helping them to patch up their differences. The executive assistant manager, Mr Dasgupta, was a great person who handled us with respect, and being at the receiving end of his humility and empathy we learned so much about the importance of carrying these traits forward. The staff in resort locations were mostly hired for the summer tourist season, so we were treated more like professionals and not summer trainees. Most of our peers who had gone to bigger properties in metropolitan cities didn't have similar experiences, nor were they given any independent responsibilities to make their jobs as exciting.

Another memorable experience during my college days was the staff strike at the Ashok Hotel in New Delhi. The strike was called by all major trade unions backed by political parties of the Opposition, who were making some unreasonable demands, the acceptance of which would have made the hotel's operations unviable. So the then management of the hotel looked for alternate staffing options. The hotel management contacted our principal for help, who thought it would be a great learning experience for the students. We were deputed to perform staff functions at the operating level, primarily the cleaning of rooms and bathrooms, providing food service and kitchen help, etc. Our involvement was a big jolt to the unions as they saw the hotel could function without them. With our support, the management broke the backbone of the staff strike, who came to the negotiating table and agreed to end the strike on the terms laid out by the management. It is another feather in Mr J.P. Sharma's cap to have had the vision to allow his students to learn from this strike. He didn't restrict our education to only textbooks and lectures and instead exposed us to the real world. We even helped with service during big conferences and banquets and by the time we left college, we were confident young individuals, equipped with reasonable, practical knowledge. This went a long way for most of us later in our careers.

I was busy with the student association for most of the year but was mostly excused for being absent from class by the faculty. By this time I had become a favourite of most of my lecturers and was allowed this privilege as they valued the work I was doing for the institute. The final examinations took place in the middle of summer, before which various hotel chains like the Oberoi Hotels, Taj Hotels, Natraj Hotel and Ambassador Hotel came to the campus for recruitment interviews. I still feel proud to have achieved this feat as a student leader since mine was the first batch to benefit from a student–staff collaboration. It may not be out of place to mention that prior to this exchange, the best job that an IHM student would get was that of a captain or receptionist at the entry level. After various rounds of my own interviews, I was selected by both the Taj Group's Indian Hotel Company as well as the state-owned and

-operated India Tourism Development Corporation (ITDC), as it was popularly called. My choice was to work for the Taj Group but in those days, as I keep pointing out, we didn't do things merely by our own choice. My father, a government employee, was extremely excited that I had been selected as a management trainee at ITDC. He gave me good counsel that a government organization was best as it provided job security and prestige, and I thus began my career in the hotel and tourism industry.

Over the next year we undertook the management training program and after another round of interviews, most of us qualified and became assistant managers. Even though our salary scales had still not been revised, I decided it was time for me to initiate my marriage plans. My parents, as I've previously described them, could not imagine having a non-Kashmiri girl as part of their family. I again used the good offices of my sister and brother-in-law to convince them that a girl with a hotel management education would be best suited to being my life partner. It would be very difficult for anyone else to understand why I needed to work long hours and regularly work till late at night. It took a few months for my parents to consent to even meeting her parents. Neelam's parents were also not keen on this alliance, but we managed to convince them to meet my parents too.

It was the month of May and my father was posted in New Delhi heading Yuv Vani, the All-India Radio youth programme. They lived in a flat provided by the government in Anand Niketan. The flat had meagre furnishings and was just adequate for my parents, who knew this was a temporary phase. Neelam helped me buy some furnishings and accessories to make the flat look more presentable. Later her parents arrived at our home in the late evening for tea. The meeting was a disaster. Both sides felt that our families were incompatible. Neelam's father was a prosperous Sindhi businessman and mine a government official.

The differences were too many, from financial to cultural. But with the divine intervention of close friends I was advised to visit Haridwar, where Neelam had returned with her family, to fight for the love of my life. My father-in-law was visibly shocked and unprepared to deal with my sudden arrival, and proceeded to lay out his concerns for his daughter's financial future and security. As a big, burly man, Neelam's father made me very nervous. He informed me that Neelam had never experienced a lack of anything and he was unconvinced as to how I would be able to provide for her. I shared that she was prepared to rough it out with me in the hopes that if we aimed for success together, we would surely find it. Eventually he couldn't cope with our resistance. I understand Neelam hadn't eaten a morsel for three days after returning from Delhi, so to my surprise, my coming to Haridwar came as a sort of relief to the family. They called Neelam down to meet me and served a high tea. I knew right then that my mission had been successful.

An auspicious date was set in the month of November for us to be formally engaged, and as I previously shared, it was a game changer moment for me because I was asked to apppear for an interview, by my superior Psyche Nigam, for a prestigious training opportunity – the Carl's Duisburg Gesellschaft Scholarship (CDG) in Germany – for which the selection process was in progress. I was interviewed and selected the very next day. The wedding was fixed to take place the following January in Haridwar.

In early November 1974, I took my first overseas journey to Frankfurt on a Lufthansa flight. A select six of us were nominated as we were already part of the mid-management of the TELCO, Steel Authority of India and ITDC by the Government of India for the Carl's Duisburg Gesellschaft Scholarship, which was an exchange programme between India and West Germany.

My wife Neelam was pregnant with our first son Amit, who was born a month later. Leaving her behind at this stage of her pregnancy was difficult for me, as was bidding goodbye to my parents. I knew that my father was to retire in March the following year. Conflicting as it was, I knew I had my own dreams to fulfil – dreams that had become closely tied to those of others close to me, who wished for me to succeed, and I for them – and I opted not to miss out on this golden opportunity. I needed this international exposure as a platform for my future success because I knew that such an experience would only help me secure a better placement later on. With a heavy heart, my companions and I boarded the flight not knowing whether we would last through the term of the training without feeling compelled to come back home instead. Two years is a long time…

On arrival in Frankfurt, we were transported to the CDG language school in Saarbrücken. Saarbrücken is the administrative, commercial and cultural centre for Saarland, Germany. The city is situated next to the French border and has a very tiny population, and although small, it has a beautiful old castle with typical European style buildings lighting up its atmosphere. We arrived in the middle of winter and it was bitterly cold for us to even think of venturing outdoors. The CDG gave us a meagre stipend of 750 deutsche marks per month. Perhaps later they realized that most of us wouldn't have our own overcoats, so they gave us extra money to purchase warm clothing. My father had given me his prized Burberry trench coat, which my uncle who lived in the US had gifted to him. So, I spent the money on other fancier winter wear.

It was my first exposure to the West. I had no knowledge of the language and was unsure of myself. Meeting with a few Indians who were engineers and managers in other fields on the same scholarship provided great comfort, as it felt great to be able to speak with people in my native language. Learning German itself was intense and kept us busy all day. The CDG sometimes took us to watch an opera at the city's beautifully old Opera Hall. Our knowledge of German was slight and I barely understood the musicals. This was our only outing and entertainment, aside from travel fairs and expos, but I did not enjoy the opera at all and wished they had shown us plays or movies instead. Food was a big issue as all our meals were predominantly German. I struggled for a long time with bland food because I didn't eat beef and pork. We used to live on bread rolls, butter, fries and lots of tomato ketchup. But after about six months I cultivated a taste for some local dishes, which I relish even now. TV channels in those days only aired programmes in German and we were deprived of any news of India. There were no mobile phones and we needed to go to the post office to book trunk calls back home. The calls took hours to materialize, that is if they did. Only on one occasion did I venture to book one. I really wanted to speak with my family about the birth of our son, but the call didn't connect. I never got to speak with Neelam or my parents even once over the phone. Our only means of communicating was letters, which took a week or more to arrive, and some of my best times in Saarbrücken were when any word from home was delivered. Finally, on completion of the language course, we were awarded our certificates in a small ceremony. To exhibit commitment to the programme and promote international relations, the then German Chancellor Helmut Schmidt came to the institution to address us. By then we knew enough German to survive in Germany, where no one spoke English at the time, even if they knew the language. The CDG also arranged for us to see some lovely places in the Black Forest area as well as the city of Heidelberg before we were to depart for our assignments at hotels and factories for the 'on-the-job' part of the programme.

The hotel I was assigned to for training was the Holiday Inn at Sulzbach, a suburb of Frankfurt. Sulzbach is a municipality in the Main-Taunus district in Hesse and part of the Frankfurt Rhein-Main urban area. The Holiday Inn there was a mid-sized hotel with about 250 rooms. The general manager Mr Peter Bierworth (known as an Innkeeper in the Holiday Inn system) met me on my first day and inquired which department

I wanted to train in. I told him that I wanted to intern under him. He was taken aback at my response as no trainee had ever been so direct with him. I explained that I was already an assistant manager back home and wanted to see myself as at least a manager of a small hotel on my return. We agreed that I would first work as an understudy to the F&B manager Mr Eichhorn and then he would consider my request, depending on the feedback he received. I already had experience running the F&B department of ITDC's Jammu Ashok Hotel, so I felt there was not much for me to learn, and I often found myself helping out by filling automats with cigarettes and soft drinks. However, my humility returned to me when I realized that I could not match the speed at which the Germans could complete a job; their efficiency was remarkable. The Germans went about their work earnestly and confidently; precision was their forte, whether it was cleaning glasses, stocking the backroom or mixing cocktails. During my initial days at the hotel I worked with the controller and in the evenings, I also worked at the bar. I was often required to help the barman wash and dry glasses. In the time that he would clean a hundred glasses, I would manage only twenty. I worked my best not to be clumsy and tried hard to catch up to his speed. Frankly I improved but never got anywhere near his perfection. I also noticed there was a lot of pilferage and short-pouring of liquor. I discussed this with the controller, who felt that putting in a security system would be more expensive than plugging the leak. I convinced him I could help and at virtually no extra cost to the hotel, I formulated a simple control system by meticulously studying how the bar staff operated.

With a pat on the back, I was moved to the Innkeeper's office as his understudy. I was finally learning new management techniques and reporting systems that were not in use in India at that time. In those day, most things in India were done in an ad-hoc manner; we were not really used to regular management information reports and actioning remedies according to them. But in Germany, there was nothing that was not structured at any of the branded hotels and other work-places. Everything in town also functioned like clockwork. You could even correct your watch at the bus stop since the bus was never even a minute late. The most important thing I've learned from the Germans is their precision and punctuality. Even today, except when genuine, I do not take it kindly when people come late to a meeting and blame the traffic for it. Mr Eichhorn and I also formed a liking for each other and became sort of friends. Unfortunately, we didn't have much means of keeping in touch and we fell out of correspondence, though I feel sorry for it.

Sometime in early April, Neelam and our son Amit, who was only four-months-old, joined me in Sulzbach. I had gone to visit my cousin brother Ashok Kachroo, who lived in Hanau, which was also a suburb but on the other side of Frankfurt. Ashok was like a local guardian to me and my only social entertainment was when I spent time with him. He fed me good Indian food at his home, which was a luxury for me at the time. I would normally take a train to Hanau and Ashok would drive me back home. On one such day past midnight as we approached the hotel, I asked him if I could stop by to check my schedule for the week. In the lobby another staff member came running to inform me that there was a telegram for me on the employee notice board. Neelam had sent it – informing me that she was to arrive by the Lufthansa flight from Delhi at 8 a.m. the next morning. As I read through the contents it was already 1 a.m. I had no transport of my own so Ashok convinced me that I should return to his house and he would drive me to the airport to receive her. The next day I saw Neelam coming down the escalator with a child fastened to her hip. This was the first time I was seeing my own son since I had not been in India for his birth. I didn't know how to react. I was not expecting Neelam to bring Amit along as I had informed her of my limited stipend. On the one hand I was thrilled to finally set my sights on him, but on the other hand I was afraid my landlady might throw us out of the house because I had not informed her that Neelam was coming with our child. Frau Hanni Faber, my landlady, acted just as I had suspected. She was angry that I had not taken her permission and gave me fifteen days to receive an objection from another tenant, in which case we would be evicted. To keep Amit from crying, we convinced ourselves to get him a pacifier when our neighbour, a night auditor who slept during the day, intimated his annoyance to Hanni. Little did we know that our paths with this person would cross again in the nineties; our neighbour became a colleague and friend at Carlson. We managed to persuade Hanni to let us stay on at Im Hol Weg, a small lane with about a dozen homes whose occupants were only local German families. On learning that an Indian family had moved in with a baby, they lined up on the street to get a glimpse of us. We had one small bedroom, barely 8 × 12 feet, near the main door. It housed one bed, which we had difficulty in sharing, a small refrigerator with a hot plate on top and a small basin next to it, which served as our kitchen sink. Under the only window was a *heitzung*, a radiator for heating. We shared the bathroom, which was outside, with other tenants. But the neighbourhood had kind people, who immediately accepted and enveloped us into their community. Help was abundant. Someone brought us a cot for the baby and Dieter Faber, Hanni's husband the landlord, provided a mattress and linen for it. We were soon comfortable in our little abode, where I finally got to eat Indian food that Neelam would cook, and it felt like home.

Our time in Germany proved to be one of the happiest phases of my life. Despite our modest living, it felt wonderful to be together with my wife and child, even with a meagre stipend of 750 deutsche marks. We stuck to bread as our staple diet, with the black *masoor dal* Germans used to make lentil soup, savouring a single cup of rice for dinner, and eating chicken once a week as a treat. In the summer, our neighbour grew knol khol. We watched her pluck it every now and then, and she would throw the leaves away. One day Neelam mustered up the courage to ask her for the leaves, which she gladly gave us. For us, it was like a special gift from God. Meanwhile, Hanni Faber became Neelam's good friend and like a godmother to Amit. Hanni helped out in more ways than we could've expected from her. She taught Neelam how to speak German and they spent their days together while I was at work; I would return home mostly after midnight on most days. She would buy clothes and baby food for Amit and even washed Amit's cloth diapers in her washing machine when she saw Neelam struggling to hand-wash them clean. Hanni was gracious enough to share her son Andrea's clothes and toys too.

Out of the tips that I earned in my days tending the bar, Neelam and I took a trip to Paris. The journey from Frankfurt to Paris was on an overnight luxury bus. Since we couldn't afford much more, we endured the bus ride without any complaint. We were housed in a small hotel with only a bidet in the room. The bathroom was outside and shared. In order to prepare powder milk for Amit we needed boiled water, but there was no restaurant or room service at the hotel. So, we went to the reception and struggled to explain to the concierge in English and gestures what we needed. All he kept saying was 'non' or 'pas'. We tried recalling some of the French we had learned at Pusa but he could not understand us. Finally, we asked him in German. Lo and behold! Within minutes we had the boiled water. We also went on a tour with my friend and his wife from my CDG days in Saarbrücken. We visited the eleventh century palace and park of Versailles, 20 kilometres outside of Paris. We became homesick walking down the Champs-Élysées because our own India Gate in New Delhi felt so similar. We visited the Eiffel Tower, the Louvre and the Notre Dame, and took a boat ride on the Seine. We took a special trip to Lido but couldn't afford the tickets, so we just took a photograph of us standing outside the building.

It's a known fact that beer is consumed in Germany like water, and the country still boasts of some world-famous brews. Even though I had worked in the bar, during my entire time in Germany I didn't once try a glass of beer, or any other alcohol for that matter. I still hadn't been introduced to the act of consuming liquor. The only exception was when we were invited to a colleague's birthday party. I was told that there would only be champagne and hors d'oeuvres. Before we left for the party, I cautioned Neelam that if she was not comfortable drinking sparkling wine, as neither of us had tasted it before, she could have it with orange juice. I had been advised that it would be very rude to refuse a drink. However, not willing to stand out she preferred to stick to the bubbly that everyone else was having. After one glass she told me in Hindi that she felt as though the room was spinning. I advised her not to consume anymore but by that time she was already a little intoxicated and kept drinking at the same pace as the rest. Luckily, we didn't need to walk too much to get home.

On one occasion, I had to leave my family alone in Sulzbach to attend some courses at the Hamburg Hotel School, a prestigious academy in Europe, where my focus was more on skill development particularly relating to F&B operations. My internship at Holiday Inn Sulzbach finished in November and I moved to the Holiday Inn Koln/Bonn Flughafen, an airport location. At Koln, I attended classes and trained further to become a good innkeeper. My initial training in Frankfurt had been at the shop-floor and supervisory level. In Koln/Bonn, the emphasis was on executive management, and I learned strategies on how to focus on overall objectives while accounting for the bottom line. So focused was I on my career that I looked for possibilities with Holiday Inn International, even though it was tough to be away from my family for so many months again. Neelam and Amit had to return to India since this time I was provided accommodation at the hotel itself. I ate staff meals, which weren't necessarily to my liking but I was happy because I shed off some excess weight. I shared the room with another supervisor who was a girl. Her name was Anya and she had a boyfriend named Mario, who was in-charge of food and beverage. It was difficult for me to share a room with a girl with whom I had no relationship, but I managed somehow. I spent my leisure hours in the gym. By the time I returned to India, I had a defined waistline. I was very fond of clothes and was able to save enough money to buy myself forty new shirts.

III

India Tourism Development Corporation (ITDC) and the Ashok Hotel

Learning to lead with a sense of self and others

In early 1982, at a little over thirty-years-old, I assumed my new post as the general manager (GM) of the Ashok Hotel in New Delhi. I never expected to be elevated to the most important operational position I could have had in my career at such an early stage. The position was usually offered to someone who was past their fifties and had enough experience dealing with the sensitivities of high-profile as well as bottom-line issues, also keeping in mind that the workings of public-sector entities were discussed and always questioned in the Parliament. In my case, I do believe it was a wonderful stroke of luck. During one of the then prime minister's unannounced visits to the hotel, she noted a few concerns and wanted to take immediate action to rectify them. The chairman and managing director decided to initiate change effective immediately and I was offered the position overnight. I was initially reluctant as many senior executives – who were expecting the promotion for themselves – put pressure on me to refuse the offer. Mr O.N. Verma, the head of corporate human resources, employed a technique of reverse psychology and implored me to turn down the offer on account that I wouldn't be able to manage a hotel of such scale. But failing was unacceptable to me, so I went ahead and accepted the challenge.

As general manager, besides operating and managing the then largest hotel in India and catering to VVIP hospitality, my responsibilities extended to Rashtrapati Bhavan, prime minister's house, Vigyan Bhawan and Hyderabad House (where select, sensitive and official entertainment took place). My key focus, besides operations and profitability, was to nurture Indian hospitality and position it at an international level. My expertise was sought in establishing Indian hospitality units internationally as well as exploring franchising opportunities. Managing and operating the business to a profit; delivering world-class standards in service; and maintaining a safe and secure atmosphere while following confidentiality protocols were an overwhelming spectrum of responsibilities, but it was particularly a privilege to oversee high-profile, highly private and strategic meetings for very select persons like Queen Elizabeth II, Yasser Arafat, Margaret Thatcher, Bob Hawke, Fidel Castro, Muhammad Zia-ul-Haq, King of Nepal, as well as presidents and prime ministers from over a hundred countries – among others.

When I took over, the Ashok Hotel was largely operated as an extended arm of the government. Some people even referred to the owner company ITDC as the Daak Bungalow Corporation. Overall staff motivation was low as people were pushed by the unions to accept unreasonable demands. Young careers were uncertain because of government policies so they remained directionless and were not supported in pursuing the right way forward. I realized the immediate need to focus more on professional training and structuring the management cadre. Higher management programmes and short courses in various verticals of hotel operations were organized in collaboration with Cornell University in the US and other esteemed institutions. We also sent people to business schools and international chains overseas to further enhance their management knowledge and skills. We no longer restricted hiring at entry management levels to hotel management graduates. Promotions from supervisory levels to management positions were encouraged to keep the staff motivated and committed. Empowering people at all responsible levels completely shifted morale and inculcated a passion to achieve more out of their work. We were also able to ignite an entrepreneurial desire in some identified rising stars. We started hiring people in key roles from outside the company. Above all, I believed in getting people who had the right kind of attitude. The motivation to hire from outside perhaps came to me from Mr Bikki Oberoi who said, 'Give me a young man from a good background with a penchant for good life, and I will make him a perfect hotelier in three years.' In my experience, this couldn't be more true.

As a leader at the Ashok, and eventually as head of the hotel division at ITDC, I did find it difficult at first to inculcate a dignity of work among most seniors at the company because of the prevalent culture in the public sector. However, as in most cases, the youth proved to be a breath of fresh air. I am particularly proud of the young assistant managers. Had it not been for them, the Ashok Hotel wouldn't have received so much acclaim by over a hundred presidents and prime ministers from around the world. These youngsters, in their twenties, led by action and achieved great heights by re-positioning the hotel and establishing some of the finest concept restaurants like Frontier, Tokyo, Burgundy, Samovar and China Town, which gave real tough competition to the likes of Bukhara. I recall taking a most difficult decision in the 1980s of asking Geeta, a young lady in the organization, to launch and manage the Garden Bar at the Ashok. It was a cultural shock for the organization but she proved to all critics that she not only set new standards but established the bar as the most hip and profitable bar in Delhi at that time. Organizational culture changed rapidly when unionized staff observed senior executives as well as young managers doing things like making up rooms, picking up chairs and personally serving guests at their tables. Such a shift had a snowball effect and most of the other ITDC hotels shortly followed suit. It was important to me that all general managers and managers at the shop-floor level felt fully empowered. The onus was on me to lead from the front.

Shortly after my appointment at the Ashok in New Delhi, I learned that the hotel was going to be the venue of two exceedingly important events in the following year. In those days, almost all foreign dignitaries and guests of the Government of India were housed by the Ministry of External Affairs (MEA) at the Ashok Hotel so it was expected that the seventh Non-Aligned Meeting (NAM) to be held in March 1983 and the Commonwealth Heads of State Meeting (CHOGM) to be held in November 1983 were going to be under my stewardship in as far as hospitality was concerned.

Historically the Ashok Hotel was among the first two five-star hotels to be built in India, but due to the uncertainty of the public sector's role over the years, modernization had taken a back step. Many processes were antique and the general atmosphere was quite passe. Meanwhile Indian hospitality had moved on and other hotels were being built and operated with modern sensibility. International events like the Asian Games, NAM and CHOGM necessitated the urgency with which the government needed to rethink the allocation of funds to modernize the hotel and its food and beverage (F&B) offerings. Our managing director Rajan Jetley impressed upon the tourism ministry and Prime Minister's Office (PMO) to let us hire international architects and designers to ensure we achieve our overall objective of a modernist overhaul.

I had no sooner stepped into my new role than the renovations of the hotel began. Seeing the potential of India's tourism and for positioning the Hotel in the international market, the internationally renowned American interior designer Dale Keller was commissioned for the project. Back in the day, Dale and his wife, Patricia Keller, were stalwarts in the field and specialized in hotel design. Some of their notable projects include the Marunouchi Hotel, the Okura Hotel and the Tokyo Hilton in Japan as well as the Hong Kong Hilton. They also restored the Taj Mahal Hotel in Mumbai and the Manila Hotel in Philippines. Dale Keller and his team transformed the somewhat decrepit Ashok hotel into a contemporary yet classic and chic space while also retaining its traditional Indian, palatial vibe.

My days were packed and my to-do list was never-ending. Rajan was a great task-master but also a great support, and although I was the youngest in his team, he trusted me the most. On many nights, long past midnight, I would trudge back to my hotel apartment along with Rajan to have dinner after the restaurants had closed. My wife and kids would be asleep, and we would microwave our dinner and talk in hushed tones about the work awaiting us the next morning. I remember he wouldn't leave till we had absolute clarity on our upcoming action items. For almost six to eight months, neither of us slept over four to five hours a night.

The pressure of the job was intense, not only because we were hosting two super sensitive international events, but also because the project department was still working on converting part of the inventory to accommodate VVIPs. The Ashok had 110 luxury and deluxe suites. Different categories of suites were created and allocated on the basis of protocol as defined by the then chief of protocol Mr Hamid Ansari, who later became the vice president of India.

Naturally, extending the quantum of work in conjunction with establishing security and safety protocols caused major delays – which blew in a force of nature to our hotel's doorstep. She was none other than the Iron Lady herself – Mrs Indira Gandhi – one of the most dominating prime ministers in Indian history.

Mrs Gandhi does not need an introduction. You know her by her sharp features, the silver streak in her hair and her crisp cotton saris. But I was privy to another side of her – a humane side, which most of India rarely got to see. She was a no-nonsense person with a great eye for details and was also quick to assess people around her. It was almost as if she could read your mind. She never forgave people for inefficiency and was rough about failure, yet she accommodated good intent. There were indeed many personalities that lay hidden within her.

Mrs Gandhi was very particular about how she deported herself in public. I remember an incident when she arrived at the hotel and I was escorting her to the banquet hall on the third floor. For a brief moment in the elevator, her personal security officer (PSO) and me were alone with her. She casually asked me about the temperature in the hall. '*Mausam kaisa hai?*' ('How's the weather?') Although I had heard her question, I simply nodded. I was lost in my own thoughts concerning the event and couldn't quite comprehend what she meant. She repeated herself to me and then got annoyed because she wanted to know whether she should drape her shawl or not. I quickly gathered myself and recommended that she wear the shawl to the event. Although the temperature in the hall was normal, neither too cool nor too warm, I didn't want to risk igniting her anger and asked our air-conditioning plant room to reduce the temperature by 4 to 5 degrees. She kept her shawl on the whole evening.

As prime minister, Mrs Indira Gandhi took a keen interest in matters concerning the country's image and became heavily invested in the preparations for NAM and CHOGM. It was naturally a mammoth task to host over seventy presidents and prime ministers under one roof at a given time. We found her turning up at the Ashok often, suddenly and unannounced, and sometimes even late at night to inspect the rooms and review the progress of the refurbishment. She would go as far as to check out the amenities and linen; she wanted to ensure that the hotel was ready in all respects to receive the dignitaries. She knew most of them personally and advised us to focus on offering personal touches where we could, and shared each head of states' likes and dislikes, the special flourishes we needed to add for each one of them, and whose suite we should allot next to whom.

March was upon us. Protocol and tradition dictate that the general manager receives all VVIPs and escorts them up to their suites. For the Non-Aligned Meeting, I received each of the dignitaries – along with Mr Daveshwar, who was in charge of protocol at the Ministry of External Affairs – at our wonderfully bedecked and fragranced reception. As a baby boomer, I belonged to a time when royalty was an actual concept, so the excitement I felt at receiving a glitterati of honourees and titles was unparalleled.

There I was, a young man privileged to be shaking hands with the likes of the Queen of Nepal – who had the softest hands I have ever shaken – Great Britain's prime minister Margaret Thatcher, and Palestine Liberation Organization (PLO) chief Yasser Arafat. Once I was asked to escort Fidel Castro, the late Cuban revolutionary, former prime minister and then president of Cuba, to his suite. When I returned to the lobby, I received a flummoxing message. I was once again asked to receive the famous Cuban president. 'I have already done so. He's in his suite as we speak,' I replied, wondering how and when he had managed to exit the hotel. That was when I was informed that the Fidel Castro I had seen to his room was a body double and the real Fidel Castro was actually at the embassy, still making his way over to the hotel. To me, the existence of a doppelgänger was straight out of a movie. Amused as I was, I quickly made myself available to receive the real person.

Our esteemed guests also brought gifts with them for the prime minister and president of India. Sometimes the gifts were cultural luxuries of great significance, other times they were a big swing and a miss, particularly when dealing with a country's local produce like a truck-load of bananas or a colossal container of musk melons. Obviously such gifts could not be taken to Mrs Gandhi. I didn't want a earful from her; on calling the Prime Minister's Office for security clearance on the items, and after consulting the Ministry of External Affairs, we decided to keep them in the holding area. Finally, we cut the fruit up into many pieces, which we distributed among the staff and even served to the guests. I remember a small tranche of fruit being sent to my apartment on a luggage trolley because it was too big to be carried up by hand.

All in all, the Non-Aligned Meeting progressed seamlessly but we had miles to go before we could sleep.

Every two years or so, the leaders of the Commonwealth nations come together for a kind of summit on a rotational basis under the aegis of CHOGM. We were still rejoicing our success with the Non-Aligned Meeting when we had to start preparing ourselves for CHOGM, which was hosted in India in 1983. This experience is among one of the most unique in my life. Besides meeting important historical figures like Queen Elizabeth II, I also learned several nuances that set the tone for the rest of my career in hospitality, particularly how to appeal to diverse cultural demands while adhering to our own protocols, which were set in place for their own reasons.

As November came marching into our calendars, I was neck-deep in responsibility of meeting our project commitments, with prime objective of providing the best service and experience to our country's esteemed guests. The days had turned cool with honeyed sunshine, the evenings crisp with the sweet fragrance of the Saptaparni trees. I hardly had time to enjoy this slide into the winter months. Soon I was shaking hands with dignitaries once again, escorting them to their rooms, pandering to their needs, and checking up on them at events.

Though I could boast of such important interactions from past experiences, I felt it was during this time that I gained keen insight into dealing with dignitaries or moguls, which has been one of the most significant takeaways of my career. One evening, as the then President Robert Mugabe of Zimbabwe was getting ready for the prime minister's welcome dinner – a banquet hosted by Mrs Gandhi for all visiting heads of state – he asked to meet me. I entered his suite, where I found him standing in his boxers, and realized he was livid. He held up a pair of trousers to my face and broke into a slew of complaints. The hotel laundry had seemingly shrunk his trousers; he had only sent them for ironing and wanted to know why they had been laundered instead. I immediately resorted to offering profuse apologies. But he was furious. He insisted he would not attend the function as he lacked the appropriate attire and would surely complain to Mrs Gandhi about this blunder. As the general manager, I knew I would have to bear the responsibility of this shortcoming and left his suite thinking a pair of trousers was going to be the end of my current post. In the worst case scenario – I thought – perhaps I would be transferred to Kovalam or some such remote location, which was customary as punishment those days at the Ashok Group. I sent for the laundry manager to ascertain the facts but he informed me that the trousers had only been ironed. How was it possible then that President Mugabe's trousers no longer fit him? I begrudgingly left for Hyderabad House where the banquet – a formal sit-down dinner that my team and I had personally worked on for weeks – was being hosted. To my perplexing relief I saw President Mugabe there, dressed in another dark suit. Even though President Mugabe would be sitting a few seats away from Mrs Gandhi, I feared he would tell her of the mishap if they got into a converzation during the pre-dinner reception. So I promptly told the staff to keep serving them hors d'oeuvres during the reception to restrict their interactions. I hoped that if he enjoyed the dinner he may forget the incident and forgive us. After all, time is a great healer. The banquet was a great success, with a wonderful meal and service by my entire team, and Mrs Gandhi was visibly happy. But I couldn't appreciate our triumph just yet. I had a sleepless night. The next morning I was summoned again to President Mugabe's suite. I entered his room feeling more nervous this time. To my surprise he welcomed me with a smile, asked me to sit and offered me something to eat. He graciously accepted that the fault lay at his end. On his way to Delhi, he had had a stopover in London where he asked Zimbabwe's ambassador to the UK to order him a dinner jacket from a well-known boutique on Bond Street. The staff at the London embassy had it collected from the shop and delivered it to the President, who didn't have an opportunity for a fitting. It was only after I had left his suite the previous evening that he noticed the size itself was incorrect. The relief I felt was unsurpassable.

Aside from a reception hosted by the Queen of England and partly organized by the Buckingham Palace team on the lawns of Hyderabad House, we managed all other events during the CHOGM. The Buckingham Palace staff and UK high commissioner in India got in touch with me to plan Her Majesty Queen Elizabeth's reception for a highly select forty couples. The UK team was boldly apprehensive about our capability to deliver an event of international class and standards, in tune with what royalty might expect. To ensure seamless preparations, they wanted to bring over some food stuff as well as crockery and napery from London – a point on which the palace authorities were insistent because their perception of Indian hospitality was one of inadequacy. Although the UK high commissioner disagreed with their impression of us, he didn't want to upset his team from London so he refrained from intervening. I protested politely but in vain. And so the Buckingham Palace staff sent forward an aircraft loaded with foodstuff and other supplies. However, just a week before the function we made a final presentation to the advance team, who pleasantly accepted our proposal at the last minute and even articulated that our planned arrangements were at par with theirs, if not better. Perhaps also not to upset the Government of India, they gave us the go-ahead we had been seeking all this while. When Neelam heard that I would have the opportunity to see Her Majesty, Queen Elisabeth II, she insisted that I take her along, even if to get just a glimpse of her. Being the baby boomers, the first crop of kids to be born in the post British Era, we were excited to even be in the same space with her. Neelam had a security pass for the Ashok hotel, which would give her entry into the Hyderabad House premises, but I couldn't promise her that she'd see the queen. She was prepared to take the risk and put on her best saree with appropriate jewels and accompanied me to the venue.

Once there, I seated her in the Managers office and proceeded to the lawns, where the reception was to be held. I told her not to leave the office under any circumstances. An hour later, however, she came running to the lawn. Seeing her disturbed me and I ran towards her wondering why would she have left the office, when I had specifically told her not to. Soon I saw the excitement on her face and a card in her hand. It so happened that we were actually invited to be presented to Her Majesty, but since the card was to be only hand delivered, and I was never available at my office, the British embassy could not deliver the card to me. A staff from the embassy finally came looking for me and asked Neelam if she knew where he could find me. She introduced herself as my wife and on seeing her security card he was relieved that he could now give the invitation card to the right person. Neelam and I felt greatly privileged to have been invited by the Queen for this exclusive event whose aim was to acknowledge the India team in charge of organizing CHOGM. I will never forget when I was presented to the Queen herself; she not only complimented me, but also regretted that she and her team had underestimated what we could deliver. She even conveyed the same to Mrs Gandhi.

The most challenging event for us was, of course, the prime minister's concluding dinner banquet, a prestigious affair of national importance, which more than seventy heads of state were to attend. Mrs Gandhi, a perfect hostess, had been personally involved in the planning of the menu, the napery, the colour scheme and other details. It was while planning this particular event that I learned a cardinal lesson in managing people. A few months earlier while we were still in the planning stages, I accompanied Rajan to a few meetings at Mrs Gandhi's residence to discuss the menu for the banquet. Since the CHOGM was being held in November, so close to Christmas, we proposed roast turkey. Mrs Gandhi gave us her approval. Then she scanned the menu with her hawk-like gaze. 'I think we should also serve biryani,' she added abruptly. 'Do you mean as an additional choice, Ma'am?' I asked. She gave me a stern look. 'No, in the same course. On the same plate.'

'But the flavours of the cranberry sauce with the roast turkey will conflict with the biryani.' She scrunched up her face and I immediately realized my mistake. She got very upset and said to Rajan, 'This is the problem with the youth of today. They are not ready to change, not ready to try out new ideas.' Rajan held my hand tight lest I went into further clarifications. The actual event flowed exactly as she had suggested, and I must confess that I had been wrong. In the eighties, I would have never suggested a fusion menu for a formal banquet but such a creative concept was really appreciated by all the guests. At the end of dinner, after the last of the guests had left and I was seeing her off, Mrs Gandhi said to me, 'I told you people will relish the combination.' A thin smile played on her lips.

My time at the Ashok Group not only helped me cultivate a sensibility towards event planning in detail and at scale, but more importantly nurtured a softer repertoire of people skills that have served me well in life and in my career. A sense of self is inevitable, and necessary, in dealing with others and when dealing particularly with VIPs, I do not suggest one should shroud away your identity. But I do urge others to follow the maxim of working smart. Think about the trade-off of arguing with a VIP. Is the argument worth one's time, effort, job? If the answer is yes to more than two of those questions, don't hold back and give it all you've got. But if not, let them have their way because at the end of the day, it will likely be a win-win for both parties. The mantra is to give the guests a good, memorable experience and be open to suggestions. This is the reality of life. What was so new to me then has turned out to be searingly popular even after thirty years. Just as in other industries, we need to continuously evolve. Thinking fondly of yesterday is only an experience but accepting changing market dynamics is the need of the hour.

Dealing with Mrs Gandhi on that particular day, as well as several other memorable interactions with prime ministers, presidents and people who matter in the government or business, I realized that to have a healthy professional relationship with anyone of their status, one has to be receptive to the client's own preferences and choices. Sometimes the suggestions may seem out-of-the-box or even ahead-of-their-time, but the key to effective execution is maintaining a flexible spirit amidst ideation. This time I asked myself – was a dinner menu important enough to argue with the prime minister of India?

Though Mrs Gandhi was a complex figure both historically and in personal interactions, I was also witness to her softer side. She hosted a very private lunch at the Rashtrapati Bhavan for then UK prime minister Mrs Margaret Thatcher during CHOGM. It was a small affair with only six attendees. While the lunch was being served, Mrs Gandhi walked upto me twice to confer whether a particular bureaucrat had eaten lunch or not. She said he had been working with her since early morning. I dutifully went to deliver her message to him both times, but the gentleman refused to eat. For some reason, she didn't relent. Instead she got up from the table, served some food on a plate and delivered it to him in the adjacent room with her own hands. The person was none other than Natwar Singh, who was working in the Prime Minister's Office in those days. I later learned that she was so concerned because he hadn't had an opportunity to eat breakfast and was starved all day.

Before I became the general manager of the Ashok in New Delhi, I began at ITDC with my first executive position in Jammu. As I've shared earlier, I moved for further studies and training to West Germany. The Government of India and the Carl Duisberg Gesellschaft sponsored me to attend a hotel school in Hamburg and train with the Holiday Inn West Germany. Upon my return at the age of twenty-five, I was given my first posting as hotel manager in Aurangabad, Maharashtra. I also had an opportunity to open a new hotel in Aurangabad and manage smaller units in Ajanta and Ellora. It may be out of context but I would like to record that it was Aurangabad where I had my first alcoholic drink, that too with Maj. Habib

Rehman then GM of Rama International. I was subsequently elevated to a larger hotel in Varanasi in the same capacity. After a successful four-year stint in Varanasi and as a part of a succession plan, I was brought in as executive manager of the Ashok, New Delhi. I had the good fortune for working under Mr Pramod Mathur whom the staff greatly revered.

During my tenure as the manager of the Varanasi Ashok, I was assigned the task of planning for the prime minister's extensive trip to Eastern UP to review progress in the state's various districts. These underdeveloped areas had no decent facilities to cater to the requirements of high-profile meetings; security and safety were also key issues even while serving the simplest food. We hired a mobile catering van and arranged for a team to travel along with her entourage to cook and serve her throughout her journey. Sunjoy Mukherjee, the then food and beverage manager at the Varanasi Ashok, led the team. I also personally went to Azamgarh, Balia and the adjacent Gorakhpur area to ensure all our arrangements were up to the mark.

I recall an afternoon when my colleague and I were sitting outside Mrs Gandhi's room and her valet Kallu Ram joined us. He was very frustrated as too many people had gathered and were hassling him for an audience with the prime minister. The then chief minister of UP Mr N.D. Tiwari, who had also joined us, affectionately held the valet's hand and urged him to divulge the madam's mood that day. Such was the fear the senior politicians had of the prime minister that anyone close to her was considered very powerful and given undue importance. I was then sent to a high-profile unionized hotel called the Airport Ashok Hotel in Kolkata, where I eventually took over as general manager and regional manager for east and northeast India. I recall an incident during our early ITDC days, when Neelam was the executive housekeeper in 1980 at our hotel the Dum Dum Kolkata. The Parliamentary Committee on Public Sector Undertakings was undertaking an inspection and Neelam had decided to help the chambermaids clean rooms as they were understaffed on account of absence of leave. Neelam never shied away from working with her own hands and did not consider any job too small for her. During an ongoing parliamentary meeting, assuming all the members of parliament were occupied, she was dusting an MP's room when he suddenly arrived to retrieve a paper from among his things. In the evening we had hosted a party for the committee, and the same MP was shocked to find Neelam at the party. On inquiring, he learned that she was the GMs' wife. He couldn't believe that in spite of her status she was assisting with groundwork such as cleaning. The next day he made a special mention of this and she received great applause from the committee.

In the year 1981, I was selected to open ITDC's newest hotel 'Samrat', from where I eventually returned to the Ashok in Delhi as general manager.

Personality can be power, I learned. And more importantly, in a world of politics, power meant everything. I recall a similar experience when Mr Rajiv Gandhi became prime minister in the late eighties. Mr Gopi Arora from the Prime Minister's Office intimated that we would be accompanying a team to Jammu to cater to a small, high-profile international delegation, who were being specially flown in to have dinner with the prime minster. The intel was confidential, and since everything had been decided at the last minute, special arrangements were made for us to transport manpower, equipment and food without haste. We arrived in Jammu in the afternoon and drove straight to the governor's house from the airport. Since Jammu & Kashmir is my home state, the governor Mr Jagmohan knew me personally. He inquired about my trip and when I mentioned the dinner, he was surprised – to my surprise. However, he asked his personal team to provide all assistance and facilitate us with whatever we needed. We were informed that the prime minister would be arriving around 7.30 p.m. while the guests would arrive at 8.30 p.m. While I was supervising preparations, Mr Gandhi walked in two hours earlier and exclaimed surprise at my presence in Jammu. I clarified I had come to oversee the dinner's arrangements. Since he had no other appointments and had come away early from electioneering, he and I strolled the lawns. We got to talking about various hospitality related matters including improvements at and the positioning of our hotels, as well as VVIP handling at Hyderabad House. His keen interest in designing new uniforms for the staff kept us engrossed and talking for a long time. In the meanwhile, seeing Mr Gandhi strolling leisurely, many people had gathered vying for his attention. But he left for his room without an audience. A local politician mistook my physical proximity to Mr Gandhi for closeness and requested me for an appointment with him, but I explained I had no such authority. He even quoted knowing my father. But despite a lack of security issues in those days – especially if one was inside an authorized zone of protocol – I knew I couldn't personally walk up to Mr Gandhi with such a request. To his luck, Mr Gandhi came out of his room and inquired on his own if there was anyone waiting to see him. I immediately called upon the gentleman, who finally got his opportunity. A few days later, this politician was sworn in as a minister in the Jammu & Kashmir Government. That same week he came to see me at the Ashok Hotel in Delhi to celebrate his appointment.

In September 1984, Zubin Mehta – ranked as one of the world's greatest orchestra conductors – came to New Delhi for the eagerly awaited Indian leg of his seven-nation Asian tour. While Mehta fulfilled yet another long-awaited ambition – to conduct the 100-piece New York Philharmonic in the country of his birth, we were busy getting ready to receive him and the members of his orchestra at the Ashok Hotel. At that time, I was corporate vice president and officer on special duty (OSD) to the managing director of ITDC, based at the corporate headquarters.

Zubin Mehta's arrival in India was not just symbolic of a return to his roots but a mark of his global success in the world of music. His handsome face had graced the covers of every major magazine in America. Apart from the Commendatore of Italy, he had been given honorary degrees from six leading universities around the world and had also received the Padma Bhushan. His tour to India received much media attention and Mrs Indira Gandhi took a personal interest in him. The hotel's executives were also excited to play host to such a famous person and hoped to receive some good media coverage too.

Each room was pre-allotted and carefully checked and equipped with VIP amenities. Upon their check-in at the hotel, the members of the orchestra were accorded a ceremonial welcome with much fanfare, including a frenzied media presence. While the check-in process was still underway at the reception, one of the musicians became hysterical and we were told that she had seen a cockroach in her room. We were baffled by the appearance of a tiny cockroach despite our meticulous preparations and attention to the minutest details. She made a big commotion and after some deliberation among themselves, the orchestra decided that the palatial Ashok Hotel was not good enough for them to stay in. The whole group, left for another hotel. All of us at ITDC were awestruck and embarrassed. Imagine a cockroach – that no one else saw – had led to such a disastrous outcome. The media, who were present in the lobby, witnessed this fiasco and found reason to make big news of it. The United News of India (UNI) and the Press Trust of India (PTI) immediately flashed the headlines. Rajan and I rushed from the corporate office to the hotel to see what we could do to retrieve the embarrassment.

The newspapers continued to carry this episode on their front pages for a few days. Mrs Gandhi became personally concerned and ordered an in-depth inquiry into the matter. She later revealed that the incident had been exaggerated as she was given to understand that some members of his troupe had wanted to go to another hotel from the airport itself. So much hue and cry had been made by the press at the behest of some interested agencies.

Thankfully the tourism ministry and the Prime Minister's Office understood the ground realities, or else some of us would have risked losing our jobs over a cockroach.

As a corporation responsible for the development of tourism infrastructure in India, with divisions other than just hotels – namely printing, publicity, sales and marketing, transport and duty-free shopping – ITDC truly served as a great training platform for those willing to learn and grow, including me.

Once I became a vice president at the corporate office, by policy I could be transferred to lead any of the corporation's divisions, and so it was that my first appointment outside of the hotels' vertical was to become the head of duty-free shopping. In those days, ITDC operated the duty-free shops at all the departure lounges of the international airports in India. I travelled extensively across domestic and international airports to study their functioning. In particular, we tied up with M/s Heinemann West Germany and involved Gustav Heinemann to lend us his expertise. I was keen to increase the breadth of our offerings and also identified the best and most appropriate vendors for liquor, cosmetics, perfumes, etc. for the Indian market. Sunil Tuli, who now heads major DFS operations in Singapore and Hong Kong, was the general manager of operations. Amidst promising growth, I became alerted to issues of major pilferage that led to duty-free goods being smuggled out of the airports and into the marketplace to be sold at a premium. But with due diligence and sincere investigation, we were able to root out the culprits. As a highlight, we opened duty-free shops in the international arrivals terminal. I am also proud to have introduced malt whisky to India and many other brands like Moulinex, Braun, etc. This phase saw the real growth of duty-free shopping in the country and was appreciated by all.

In addition to my existing responsibility, I was also given the charge of ITDC's sales and marketing division, which also coordinated the marketing initiatives for most of the state governments.This post was particularly dynamic and exciting, and as has been the nature of my tenure with the company, I got to meet many people from all walks of life. I also had the privilege of facilitating many strategic tie-ups on behalf of this public sector organization, which included agencies, like Trust House Forte – UK and Golden Tulip.

I recall a fond incident when the then chairman Mr Ram Laxman asked me to meet and entertain his guest – a Mrs Marilyn Nelson. When we met for lunch, she informed me that she was the head of the Carlson Group's Wagonlit Travels – the world's largest travel company – which is when I also learned that Carlson had various businesses other than hospitality. Little did I realize that I'd be working for her one day.

After these successful assignments, I finally became head of ITDC's hotels' division, gaining invaluable experiences that proved useful to me even in my later days at Carlson Hotels/ RHG (Radisson Hotel Group).

Working in the public sector poses a unique set of challenges, particularly in dealing with influential and often difficult people. Over the years, I've found myself in the middle of many storms, some that possess so much humour on looking back though in the moment the consequences felt grave. As I mentioned, one of the key takeaways of my time working in the public sector has been developing a keen understanding of other people – their dispositions, moods, personal contexts – and as a result, I also groomed a strong sense of self.

When dealing with high-profile persons like dignitaries and famous people, I've learned it is natural to become unnerved or feel out of your comfort zone but it is important to remember that they are people after all. Staying calm is your biggest asset because you will be better equipped to understand what they are demanding from you in the moment. A calm head is worth its weight in gold. Whatever you do, do not become aggressive in stance, body language or words. Aggression or passive aggressiveness will only make the situation worse. It's surprising how many of us spend more time formulating our replies than listening. Just like public speaking, active listening is an art that when practiced will improve in time. When it is important to stick to a stand that you're confident will enhance your professional space, a firm and polite tone will get your work done over a boorish attitude. It can be tempting to explain and justify your actions while problem-solving but people are more receptive to solutions, so think about solutions you can offer and present them in a polite manner.

Most importantly, there is a subtle but great difference between ego and pride. Approaching a task or situation with your ego is when you are set in your ways and think that you are right no matter what the context. On the other hand, when you are proud of what you do, where you work and the people you work with, you will naturally want the best for your company or brand. Remember you will frequently need to make decisions based on how they will affect your brand more than you.

IV

Leaving the Public Sector

Philosophy is the knowledge of how you live life

It's no surprise that money is a powerful motivator, especially for people to change their jobs, sometimes even their careers. But this was not true for me – at least at first. In my thirties, I was heading a few verticals at ITDC, including an operating portfolio of over forty hotels. I loved my job and overall I was a happy, contented person. We lived in a big suite at the Samrat Hotel. My children, wife and mother were equally happy in their own lives. My colleagues, subordinates and employees respected me. All was more than well.

In 1990, things changed. All of a sudden I had a new boss, a senior IAS officer – a bureaucrat – who wanted to exercise exclusive control over the corporation. He seemed unsure of entrusting too much control to me; I had already been in the company for almost two decades and had a very inclusive management style. He often doubted my decisions, and what bothered him most was that any orders he gave to my colleagues and subordinates resulted in them routing those instructions through me, as if to check back, before taking action. This informal chain of command understandably alienated our relationship. He remained unconvinced by the support I garnered within the organization. He even went to the extent of doing special favours for some young executives to win over their loyalties, but these strategies failed. I found such working conditions difficult but I was somehow able to tide over this time by diligently carrying on with my work.

Then, to make matters worse, a new minister for tourism also entered my life. He would call me to his official home in Lutyens' Delhi and some of his staff gave me orders that I found difficult and even impossible to implement. For example, they had a vested interest in placing a certain cohort of people at executive levels and urged me to employ them, but there were hardly any available positions and their list of recommendations was too large to even attempt. Besides, there was a protocol to follow and they expected me to ignore it, but my conscience wouldn't allow me to follow through. The minister also made a TV announcement – without prior discussion or written communication to us – that anyone who came to an ITDC hotel in a *dhoti*, essentially farmers, would get a room for less than half the normal tariff and 50 per cent discount on food. We waited to receive orders in writing but they were never issued. So when flocks of non-mainstream clientele landed up in *dhotis* at our five-star properties across the country, demanding stays at that tariff, the general managers refused to let rooms out to them. The minister's office tried to directly pressurize some general managers but they still refused to comply.

Incidents like these led to my falling out of favour with his office. Prior to his appointment, I had been shortlisted by the Public Enterprises Selection Board (PESB) for the position of the next managing director of the company. But the ministry did not want me to get that position, preferring to have someone of their own choice in a position of command.

In early April 1991, an unexpected event occurred that changed the course of my life. Although at that time I felt that the stars were no longer in my favour, I now believe that it was destiny (and no other reason) that was actually carving a new path for me. Only I couldn't see it at that time. There had to be a reason for me to change the path I had travelled on so far. One evening, I was ready to leave for a family wedding at the Maurya Sheraton in New Delhi when the doorbell to my apartment rang. My personal helper had taken our dog for a walk so I opened the door instead. In the corridor I found our security guard grasped by two tall, big-built men. One of them spoke gruffly. 'Who is Kachru?' His boorish tone of voice only added to my suspicions, aroused at first by the security guard's nervousness. The guard hesitantly explained that he had tried to stop the men from coming up to my room but they had not listened to his pleas. Luckily hotels have self-locking systems and I immediately shut the apartment door behind me. The two men introduced themselves to me as police officers. One of them claimed he was a station house officer (SHO) in-charge of a police station and presented his identity card. I imagined it may be a CBI search and asked for a warrant. They had none but were still insisting for access to the apartment. They said a murder had taken place and they believed the weapon was hidden in my apartment. They demanded to inspect the premises. I found the courage to yell at them. I am a peace-loving man and normally never raise my voice in anger, but on this occasion I was so insulted because I knew they had the wrong person. It seems I did manage to intimidate them because I also managed to lead them down to the lobby, away from the apartment, where I felt safer knowing more executives and hotel security personnel were presant. They followed me but also assumed I might try to run away so they said I'd be shot if I tried to escape, since many police cars were surrounding the hotel.

Being the head of a hotel chain belonging to a public sector undertaking, I was well connected. I knew the home minister personally, as well as senior police officers and other ministers, mostly from previously undertaking security preparations at the Ashok Hotel for various foreign dignitaries. Those days there were no cell phones but I had a great memory for numbers. I managed to make my way to one of the desk phones in the lobby, from which I called the home minister – but he was not at home. So next I tried the home ministry's secretary, but he was also not available, and nor was any other senior police official I could think of on the spot. When I finally got through to the officer on special duty (OSD) to the home minister, he was equally amused and shocked at my situation. He was certain I had nothing to worry about and said he would sort out the matter, but the police official refused to take his call. Meanwhile, the minister's OSD told me not to worry as he was sending a message to the control room over the police wireless. To my great relief, the policeman and cars vanished within minutes of the transmission.

However, I was still rattled. Later that evening, we called our friend Navin Berry, who is a well-known journalist, and went over to his home for drinks and dinner. When I conveyed the story to him, he believed it to be more than a case of mistaken identity and advised me to report the matter to the secretary of tourism. I took his advice and decided to formally raise the issue. When I spoke to the secretary of tourism, he asked me to make a written complaint. I did, and then called on the principal secretary to the prime minister – who had previously been my boss – and he assured me that there must be some misunderstanding. Although nothing was officially revealed, I had managed to clear my name while also learning certain facts that left Neelam and me in a state of shock. The police officer who had come to search our apartment was himself being questioned for several issues. It was not unusual those days to hear the stories of planting unauthorized substances and then to 'discover' them on site. Fortunately I had closed the apartment door from behind during our interaction as a result of which even if they wanted, they could not have entered the premises.

Naturally, we were still afraid. Even if I wasn't guilty, I was battling torment and confusion. I couldn't understand how or why anyone would try to frame me in a murder case and I was worried about tarnishing my reputation. As a family, we agreed that it was no longer safe for me to work here and that it may be better for all of us to even move out of the country. And so I was compelled to take the extreme step of quitting a safe and secure government job as I could not risk continuing on under compromised circumstances, with the safety of my family and my reputation at stake. I was left with no option except to look for an opportunity overseas since it was unlikely that the private sector would employ me because of political reasons. Leaving ITDC was an unplanned decision, so I had no real offer in hand but I could also not afford to be jobless as I had the responsibilities of growing children, an aging mother and my wife too, who was no longer employed. I had negligible savings so I needed a job as soon as possible to maintain my children's education and household expenses, forgetting luxury as a concept, which our family had grown used to by staying in hotel suites all along my career at ITDC. I realized that all these years I had worked primarily for the perks, since my government salary left me with hardly any savings and assets. I did have a nicely renovated DDA flat in Vasant Kunj, but I had a bank balance of only a little over Rs 1 lakh. In addition, moving to a DDA flat from a huge five-star deluxe hotel suite would not have been an ideal change to any of us. Thus, deciding to resign was not an easy decision at all, because my position at ITDC afforded me not only a comfortable life but also one that was prestigious and the envy of many at the time. Despite the precarity of my situation and all the uncertainty it brought with it, I could not rationalize the fear I felt on being falsely implicated in a murder. Had it not been for the panic I felt, I would never have been able to take this step.

That same evening I received two calls. One was from my father-in-law, who had specifically called to ask if all was well with us, as he didn't have a good feeling. I didn't want to share this information with him and put my wife's family under stress. The other call was from Singapore, from Rajan Jetley. Rajan had had a premonition that all was not well at my end. I burst into tears. When I told him the whole story, he was very kind and assured me that he would help in any way I needed. I am also grateful to a few of my bureaucrat, parliamentarian friends and an ex-minister of state for tourism, who went out of their way to provide mental and emotional support during this most difficult period of my life.

Meanwhile, I also sought advice from some of my mentors. I am grateful to Mr S.K. Misra, who personally accompanied me to meet with the Deputy Prime Minister and clarify my innocence and position despite being such a busy man. Subsequently, the minister assured me of his full support. His OSD felt that he may have been misguided. But after such a sordid experience, I had made up my mind to leave the public sector and resigned the very next day. The dilemma then grew to how I would proceed with searching for another job. Neelam reminded me that Juergen Bartels, or J.B. as he was known, the president of Radisson Hotels International, had offered me a position in the past. I had declined the offer at the time since I was – as I like to reiterate – happy, and had no wish to relocate to the US. But even so, he had told me to contact him whenever I was ready for a change. After much persuasion from Neelam I called him around midnight in Delhi, which was 12:00 p.m. in Minneapolis. I informed J.B. that I had left ITDC and that he was the first person I'd thought to contact. After exchanging some pleasantries, he told me to wait for his call the next morning, but it was difficult for me to sleep because I was anxious about his decision. J.B. was to consult with Curt Carlson, the chairman and owner of Carlson companies. However, to my delight, he called back within twenty minutes to let me know that my job search was over and that he would discuss the modalities later.

I served a notice period at ITDC and then left for Singapore. Some months later, a relative of the minister's visited and we had lunch. He expressed concern over what I had had to endure. Later, when I returned to India he even offered me help. To this day, we wish each other well.

Carlson's assignment expected me to relocate to Singapore. Therefore, in April 1991, Neelam and I took a short trip to Singapore to arrange the children's school admissions and lease an apartment. Later in July, we boarded an Air India flight to

Singapore taking with us our clothing, silk Kashmiri carpets, silverware and artworks for the house. We had leased a furnished apartment from a very sophisticated, good looking and gentle Pakistani lady named Rosie Zaman. We were fortunate to get a three-level duplex flat, which felt more like a house, with four bedrooms. It was well-lit and airy overlooking Grange Road, which is a few minutes' walk from Singapore's busiest boulevard called Orchard Road. For a few days we stayed with the Jetleys in their home until we moved into our own abode, which gave both the families, including the children, the opportunity to reconnect. Rita Jetley, Rajan's wife, assisted us with procuring necessary household items and helped us in every way to settle in.

My family was excited to be in Singapore and we spent the first month exploring the city together. We were cautious about the stringent rules in the country, especially regarding driving and parking. It would still get lonely at times, but before we realized the festival of Diwali arrived. While we missed the large-scale celebrations Delhi had to offer, soon Rita and Rajan introduced us to their social circle and we made a lot of good friends through them. Thereafter we were busy most evenings, visiting others or entertaining guests at home. Sumithra, our Sri Lankan house-maid single-handedly did the work that a number of helpers could have completed back in Delhi. She ensured we were always comfortable and pampered us with good home-cooked food.

The biggest change I experienced was in the office environment, where only Rajan, a secretary and I worked. On my first day, Rajan asked me if I'd like to have tea. My reply was, 'Yes, of course.' Then he took me to a corner outside his office, which had a big kettle, tea bags, etc. He said, 'Today I will teach you how to make your tea. Going forward, you can make your own tea and give me a cup too!' We both laughed because in India we had a retinue of staff to do all our chores. This was a different world. But soon enough the strangeness of a new place transformed into home.

Spiritual Blessings

His Holiness Dalai Lama

Sri Sri Ravi Shankar

Laying Foundation Stone of D-Bhawan
at Mata Vaishno Devi Shrine

Santoshi Mataji

Ma Anandamayee

Dignitaries

Bob Hawke, Australian Prime Minister

Robert Mugabe
President of Zimbabwe

Secretary General, United Nations

The President of Guyana

Dignitaries

Zial-ul-Haq, President of Pakistan with his Begum

Fidel Castro, President of Cuba

Birendra Bir Bikram, King of Nepal

Jigme Singye Wangchuck, King of Bhutan

Gen. Hussain Muhammad Ershad, President of Bangladesh

Junius Richard Jayewardene, President of Sri Lanka

Dignitaries

The President of Algeria

The President of Jamaica

HH Amir of Qatar

Head of State of Kenya

Dignitaries

Margaret Thatcher, Prime Minister of the United Kingdom

Shridath Ramphal, Secy. General, CHOGM

Eminent Leaders

Indira Gandhi

Rajiv Gandhi and General Sethna

Neelam Sanjiva Reddy,
President of India

Rajiv Gandhi

Atal Bihari Vajpayee

Sports Personalities

Kapil Dev, Indian Cricketer

Syed Kirmani, Indian Cricketer

Holding World Cup Trophy with Sunil Gavaskar, Indian Cricketer

Mary Kom, World Boxing Champion

Sir Edmund Hillary, First Mountaineer to Climb Mt. Everest

Geet Sethi, World Billiard Champion

Brand Promotion

Launch of Country Inns in India, Anil Kapoor, Bollywood Actor

Madhuri Dixit, Bollywood Actor

Salman Khan, Bollywood Actor

Launches

Launch of CDMS - Country Development and Management Services

TGI Fridays Launch in India

Launch of Radisson and Colony Hotels in Malaysia

Signing of Park Inn & Suites Deal

Opening of
'The Great Kabab Factory'

Proud Moments

Rakesh Sharma and Ravish Malhotra, India's First Two Astronauts

Honoured by S.D. Sharma
President of India and
N.T. Rama Rao, CM, Andhra Pradesh

Mukesh Ambani

Ratan Tata

V

Carlson Hospitality and the Radisson Hotel Group

Predict your own future by creating it

With renewed support, Rajan Jetley and I set up 'Radisson Hotels Asia', a company that had development rights for the whole of Asia, except China. Neelam and I were excited that my older son Amit got admission at the International School of Singapore and Sameer was admitted to United World College and both would receive a world-class education.

Rajan Jetley set up an office at a prestigious address on Orchard Road. Although, no one had heard of Carlson or its brands in this region, Rajan and I continued our operations in Singapore with notable fervour. We both knew Tunku Iskandar, the chairman of Melawar Corporation, who had also been the chairman of the Pacific Asia Travel Association (PATA). Besides being from the royal family of Malaysia, Tunku was a renowned figure in the travel trade in the region. Carlson's upper midmarket brand in those days was 'Colony Hotels & Suites' and we managed to tie up with Tunku's Melawar group to develop a few Colony hotels in Malaysia and Indonesia. We also signed other properties under the Radisson brand with leading industrialists and developers of the region. Our key investors included the Salim Group of Indonesia. We were also lucky to sign an ultra-luxurious resort property in Langkawi with the then chairman of Malaysian Airlines. Our partners in Indonesia, Malaysia and Thailand were quick in building or converting their existing hotels to the Radisson brand. Most of these hotels started operating within eighteen to twenty-four months of signing contracts. This gave the Radisson brand huge visibility and we started moving into newer territories. We signed key hotels in Surabaya, Bali, Jakarta, Bangkok and Kuala Lumpur.

We didn't have the resources at the time to operationally manage these hotels so we focused on signing only franchise deals. Carlson had a tie-up with David Boward of Radisson Hotels in Australia to manage their franchised properties there and so his company was entrusted with the responsibility of managing Radisson properties in Indonesia as well. We also created a joint venture with Prarob Mukawis, ex-president of the Regent Hotels, Thailand for managing our properties in Thailand. Carlson soon nominated a senior official, Jack Geddes to coordinate the growing scale of sales and marketing for our hotels in the region. Things were looking good by 1994.

However, the ASEAN markets suddenly saw one of the worst economic downturns in late 1995. With stock markets and general numbers on the decline, investors were shying away from investing in real estate, which adversely affected our next phase of development since hotels typically have longer gestation periods than other commercial projects. It is at this stage that we reviewed our strategy. While continuing to work in the ASEAN markets, we started focusing more on South Asia, which was mostly possible with the guidance and constant support of Jim Olson who oversaw development for Radisson International in the Asia-Pacific. He was swift and sharp to understand the different cultures and customs of Asia and the diversity in its work styles and ethics. He believed in 'acting local while going global', and nurtured the team to achieve our next set of goals keeping such nuances in mind.

Given the company's reluctance to invest in real estate, provide minimum guarantees or take properties on lease, the only option available to us was to identify strategic partners and share the benefits of growth together. Carlson chose the joint venture and representation route to specifically enter the South Asian market though the development of new brands remained a more uphill task. Even in mature markets like Singapore, significant opportunities came our way but because of company policy not to invest in real estate, we lost out to others who were prepared to seed the market with minimal investments or provide minimum guarantees.

However, despite certain policies whose efficacies are debatable, we were encouraged to work outside our territory since the company was still small and flexible. Not many people are aware that Radisson Hotels Asia was instrumental in bringing the Radisson Lexington Hotel, New York, and Radisson Hotel, Mauritius, into the company's fold. Radisson Hotels Asia was also responsible for bringing Carlson's restaurant brands TGI Fridays and Italianni's to Singapore, Malaysia, Indonesia, Japan and later to India, but more on this later. During his first press conference in Singapore in 1991, J.B. announced that the company would brand at least forty hotels in a span of four years. I had no idea how I would achieve this target. But he turned to me and said, 'It is you, K.B., who will make this a reality.' We actually achieved all this in a span of five years. J.B. had been right, and my respect for his vision grew even more.

In 1995, with the onset of new liberalization laws India began to open up its economy. There was a huge gap in the demand and supply of hotel rooms in the country, which is precisely when real-estate barons decided to invest in developing hotel properties. They had the resources and were masters of construction business but had little or no know-how in operating hotels. They needed hotel management companies and reputable brands to operate their hotels for them. Even while being based in Singapore, I made at least forty trips to India to pursue the opportunities available in the country at that time. Between my travels around Asia and back and forth to India, I was constantly on the move. Neelam often joked and called me a resident of no country.

With the company's strategic pivot I decided to return to India, my motherland, to aggressively pursue the growth of Carlson's brands in South Asia. I realized the future of my career depended on my ability to take the risk of coming back, and it was another crucial juncture at which to test my own strengths. India was supporting growth and positivity and all of us realized it, including Neelam, who whole-heartedly supported the move.

Carlson formed a joint venture by the name of Scotts Carlson, with Scotts Holding, a company headquartered in Singapore, to primarily develop hotels pan India under the Country Inns & Suites by Carlson brand (CIS). I was offered to head this joint venture as managing director. I set up an office at the Qutab Hotel in Delhi, which was an ITDC Hotel at the time. I even stayed at ITDC's Samrat Hotel for six months while my own house was being renovated. Scotts Holding had procured large chunks of land in Gurgaon, in what is currently known as Sushant Lok 3, to develop a mix-use colony, offering service apartments, hotels, commercial and residential complexes. That same year the Jumabhoys, who controlled Scotts Holding, had a family dispute and the Government of Singapore took over control of the company, changing their priorities and going slow on the India investment plan. The then chairman of Scotts Carlson India, Mr Ramesh Sarin (of ITC and Carrier fame) was indeed very kind to have helped get the company to adequately compensate me. It was a difficult phase for me personally as I had to provide for both my sons' education overseas. My older son was pursuing an undergraduate degree in Texas, and my younger son was studying at the United World College in Singapore.

Once again I was uncertain about what security I held, what the future had in store for me. It was one of the few times I was driving my car through Delhi's serpentine traffic because my driver was on leave that day. I was feeling disheartened as Scotts Carlson, the joint venture with whom I had moved from Singapore back to India, was shutting shop. I may have been driving but it was my mind that was in overdrive. I looked up from the steering wheel and realized I had two options – I could look through the windscreen or the rear-view mirror, just as in life. A windscreen looks forward, offering an unlimited horizon and the capacity to take one to unknown places and heights, whereas a rear-view mirror is much narrower in view and roots you in looking back. And the past was past. I needed to cut my losses since the best I could do was look onto the next thing. I was invigorated with the inclination to rebuild my present and my focus shifted to a more promising future. All of a sudden I was so positive I felt I might even foretell the future.

Rajan and I had not closed Radisson Hotels Asia, which was still based out of Singapore. So I decided to give up the office that I had leased at Qutab Hotel for Scotts Carlson and start afresh. To focus all efforts in developing Carlson hotel brands, I set up a new office at the yet-to-open Radisson Hotel, Mahipalpur, which soon came to be known as the Carlson Hotels Development Office, with me as the head. Neelam, who was not pursuing anything professionally at this time, showed a keen desire to work with me. Neelam has always had a keen sense of observation and tended to take a deeper interest in our hotel interiors and the changes they would undergo from time to time. Since she is very creative, I have relied on her to come up with innovative and cost-effective ideas at the office, especially in the days when resources were scarce. She has been a great support to me throughout my time in the development business while at Carlson. We put together a small, multi-tasking team; a secretary, an IT person, and Sarbir an office boy is all we could afford. Incidentally Sarbir is still with us and serves with devotion. As a team, we initially added about fifty hotels to Carlson's portfolio of brands, which included Regent, Radisson, Park Inn, Park Plaza, and Country Inns & Suites by Carlson. One of the first hotels we signed in South Asia was the Radisson Water Garden Hotel in Dhaka, Bangladesh. Negotiations were held at the level of the army chief since the land belonged to the state and investment in the hotel was part of the army pensioner's fund. This deal was a challenge in itself, and had it not been for Masud and Pintu, our local associates, the deal would never have happened. The Radisson Water Garden Hotel has remained one of the largest fee-earners for the company in the region. We simultaneously signed a hotel in Nepal.

Initially we reported directly to Jim Olson at Carlson's headquarters in Minneapolis. He was the person, who actually understood and created Carlsons' presence in Asia-Pacific. It was only much later that Carlson sent Paul Kirwin to Singapore to head the Asia-Pacific office, which was relocated from Sydney, considering how far away it was from the rest of the region. Meanwhile, Jim Olson had an unexpected seizure on returning home from a jog and sadly passed away at the age of fifty-six. Paul would visit India often and I was required to visit Singapore at least once every quarter. After a few years, Paul was recalled back to the US. Since then, our Singapore headquarters has seen a few CEOs, namely Jean Marc, Simon Barlow, Thorsten Kirschke and Katerina Giannouka, who was the last president of the Radisson Hotel Group in the Asia-Pacific. RHG South Asia now reports directly to the global head office in Brussels.

My move to India had been centered around developing Carlson's mid-segment brand Country Inns & Suites, but given the set-back to our strategic partnership with Scotts Holding, we were wrangled into reviewing our growth plans. The company asked me to focus on the development of its other hotel and restaurant brands, including Radisson and TGI Fridays, but India was practically a virgin market for franchising and I felt that the management and distribution of hotels was the future for the industry. And so, we re-strategized our priorities.

Since Carlson was still not ready to make any real-estate investments in the region, I started looking for strategic partners as I had done in Singapore. Radisson Hotel Mahipalpur, owned by AB Hotels, was the first hotel we signed in India. Unitech and AL Batra Group were our partners in the deal and it was

Psyche Nigam, a previous boss at ITDC, who had introduced them to me while I was still in Singapore. In 1996, it is thanks to Dr Shrivastav's support, and Mr Luther's support, when Radisson Hotel Mahipalpur was still under construction, we set up a development and liaison office on the hotel premises. Working in India offers unique experiences. We were using the Internet at the office to send out emails, which was comparatively still a new concept in the country, and in contrast we would see bricks being transported on donkeys to the construction site. It was amusing to see the world around us changing – but only that much. The hotel was due to open in 1996 and the then prime minister Mr Deve Gowda was to come for the inauguration. Staff had been hired and trained for almost six months. Invitation cards were printed and distributed. Then what we least expected, happened. The hotel didn't receive the necessary permissions to operate from the government authorities for reasons beyond our comprehension. It seems separate authorities had gotten into a controversy as to who would be the licensing authority. Consequently inauguration was stalled as was the opening of the hotel. Though the owners commendably retained all their staff, everybody was demotivated because uncertainty loomed for almost two years. The hotel finally opened for business in 1998 and was a grand success from the day of launch. A lot of the credit goes to Sanjiv Tyagi, the hotel's first vice president and general manager, for establishing high standards of service and offering guests a unique experience. Many of my colleagues from the industry had said that the location would be a disadvantage for us, but our proximity to the airport and Gurgaon, where there were no branded hotels, became a plus point. Moreover, restaurants at the Radisson, especially The Great Kabab Factory, were an immediate and necessary pull for guests.

Meanwhile, I was simultaneously looking around for opportunities for Country Inns & Suites by Carlson. Having previously served as an advisor to the Jammu and Kashmir Tourism Development Corporation, I contacted the then chief secretary Mr B.K. Goswami. He took me around Katra to identify a piece of land where an upmarket, mid-scale hotel could be developed for pilgrims and also serve as a resort getaway for people in the Jammu region. Mr Goswami was also instrumental in introducing me to Mr Dev Mohan Gupta and his family, who were potential investors and themselves keen on developing facilities for pilgrims visiting the Mata Vaishno Devi shrine. It is a sheer coincidence that the government later appointed me to the board of the shrine, along with Sri Sri Ravi Shankar and Mr Vijay Dhar. This temple receives around 9 million pilgrims a year. We identified a beautiful site about 7 kilometres from Katra city, with a view of the hill leading up to the shrine. The site had been rejected by most other developers, who thought it was too isolated from the rest of the city, but it was precisely why I thought a premium brand would work here, away from the hustle and bustle of the city centre. The land belonged to local farmers and it took us around a year to consolidate and procure it and also get necessary government approvals. And so we signed our first Country Inns & Suites by Carlson in India. Paul Kirwin, who was the president of CIS Hotels with its worldwide corporate office in Minneapolis, became personally involved in the deal. When the question arose of who would manage the property, Peter Blyth, president of development at Carlson Hotels Worldwide, offered Rajan and me the opportunity to set up our own management company. By now I had spent a great deal of time involved in day-to-day operations and was intrigued by an umbrella view focusing on growing these international brands not only in metropolitan cities but also tier-1 and tier-2 towns. I was no longer interested in operating hotels and was enjoying development and franchising.

While I was still scouting around for a strategic local partner, Shiv Jatia – owner of the Hyatt Regency Delhi – and his partner Ranjan Bhattacharya were also looking to set up a management company and tying up with an international brand. Ranjan is a trained hotelier and previous general manager at the Oberoi Group of Hotels. When they contacted Carlson Hotels Worldwide, Jim Olson asked me to pursue the conversation.

We were thrilled; we quickly realized we had found the right people for us, with Shiv being the owner of the very happening Hyatt in Delhi and Ranjan being an astute hotelier, who is also the son-in-law of the late and well-respected Mr Atal Bihari Vajpayee. After several meetings and negotiations, their company Chanakya Hotels was awarded the master franchise to develop the Country Inns & Suites brand in India and manage our operations. We set up a joint venture called Country Development & Management Services (CDMS) with an office in Greater Kailash in Delhi, and I was nominated by Carlson to serve on its board. Ranjan was appointed as MD of CDMS and Sanjeev Pahwa was designated as head of operations and Atul Jain looked after the finance and administration. The Katra CIS hotel, which had been directly signed by the parent company, was handed over to CDMS to operate. Because the company was still growing and there were limited resources, initial technical services were provided by M.L. Bhattacharya, who was the project head for Radisson Blu Plaza Hotel, Mahipalpur, at the time. Our collaborative development strategies enabled CDMS sign multiple locations and open over thirty hotels.

With a reasonable number of hotels under development across Carlson brands, we then felt a pressing need to initiate a definite structure for sales and marketing to not only give visibility to our brands but also to translate our growth targets into accommodated hotel rooms. Our resources as well as revenues continued to be limited during this period, so we outsourced these critical functions to Talent Marketing India operated by Pankaj Kodesia, who really drove the company forward. The company was owned by Shiv and Ranjan. He helped us appropriately chart out the positioning for our various brands and generate reasonable business after we opened our hotels. However, we realized that outsourcing such critical functions could only be a short-term arrangement, so we proposed they partner up with us to set up Carlson Hospitality Marketing India Pvt. Ltd. (CHMI) – funded by part of the marketing fees collected from franchisees in South Asia, the rest of which was used for international marketing. But even so, these funds were not enough to support CHMI's operations, which included the setting up of a centralized reservation office or toll-free call centre. It was imperative that we cover important hubs in India by setting up regional sales offices in Delhi, Mumbai, Bangalore, Kolkata and Chennai, and I managed to convince owners and executives of the economies of scale that we would benefit from should we collaborate on these collective initiatives. With unanimous agreement, Carlson Hotels India Nepal Sales & Marketing (CHINSAM) was formed, which was funded by each hotel owner in conjunction with the number of rooms they had, over and above their marketing fees. All sales and marketing activities were governed by the board, which consisted of seven members – four hotel owners and three Carlson nominees. I personally oversaw CHINSAM's operations for many years. Ranjan's and Dr Kapur's inputs were immense to make CHINSAM a success.

What started out as a unique alternative to a budgetary constraint ended up resulting in our expansion in the region, deepening and blossoming inter-relationships among various hotel representatives. In fact, CHINSAM became so popular that the owners and general managers of our hotels agreed to participate in other collaborative events and initiatives such as an annual cricket tournament, known as Super Sixes, which was held in Delhi for many years. The Carlson Cup League, as it was called, was like a mini premier league event replete with sponsors, music and cheerleaders. India was the only country where all of Carlson's company verticals and brands got together, Carlson Wagon Travel who were not even part of the hospitality group. Employees and executives from all over the country would greet and mingle at these hosted dinners and every year, the president of Carlson Asia-Pacific would come from Singapore to give out awards. Other HR initiatives included bar-tending and bakery – confectionary contests.

By early 2000, we had a similar understanding vis-à-vis operations and in this case we realized we couldn't piggy-back for much longer on other Radisson properties in our development of new hotels. We needed to establish a local management company that could provide services to our operating hotels and also conduct regular product quality reviews. I was personally still hesitant to get back into operations, and I did not want to set up an infrastructure of my own, so once again I searched for a strategic partner to manage our Radisson and select Park Plaza hotels. Our first choice was the parent company of Radisson Delhi, AB Hotels, who owned the flagship hotel and were building two more. Carlson was keen that I be personally involved in the company – to ensure my long-term commitment – so Radisson Hotels Asia, which Rajan and I owned, took some equity in this new strategic venture that we called RHW Management Services. Special gratitude goes to Dr Ramesh Kapur for supporting our activities. He helped us in all possible ways, including giving us office space at a highly subsidised rate, allowed his hotel executives to work for RHW pro bono and even served free lunches to our executives. It is on account of these shared services that RHW not only survived but also grew at this stage. We grew steadily, from a lean staff to more and more management and franchise contracts. We were now able to offer standardized experiences in our hotels in the region, and better control hotel standards – from acquiring talent to training them to identifying vendors at attractive rates and standardizing amenities. Rajan Narula and Rupinder Garg CFO's of RHW deserve all the credit to create and manage the structure to the satisfaction of all stakeholders. It was their ingenuity that enabled RHW to support itself from the very first year. Nilesh Mitra too did a fantastic job as our head of human resources. With our hotels enjoying economies of scale too, our guests could be certain of what to expect at any Radisson property they visited, which is a hallmark moment in the service industry.

RHW soon became an established management company in India, but I must mention the challenges we faced in obtaining talent at that time when most hotel management graduates in India preferred to join as management trainees – but we had no such programme. The Taj Group, Oberoi's and ITC were our main competition and they all ran their own management training programmes as well as hotel schools.

To ramp up our abilities in servicing our managed and franchised hotels, we needed to assist our properties with getting the required trained manpower. Resources were scarce, Neelam has also been known to employ untrained staff with good attitude and take up the task of training them herself. I recall a time when she was not technology savvy and was learning how to work with computers but was teaching her staff alongside. Of course, in the end they mostly excelled. She started her career as a teacher while at IHM Pusa, from when on her teaching skills have been one of her strengths. It has given her great satisfaction to see a lot of the people that she trained now hold senior management positions. She has also helped many children from among our family and friends with their studies. Moreover, in her free time, revering it as a social welfare activity Neelam has even taught the household staff to speak English and some of their children too because of which they now have more respectable jobs. Given the situation, we decided to establish our own hotel management institution. I spoke with Curtis and Marilyn Carlson Nelson, who represented ownership at Carlson Companies, and they agreed to contribute to the cause that would support their business activities in India and globally as well. They even established multiple scholarships at IHM pusa in my name to recognize our efforts to develop talent till we operationalize our school.

I asked Unitech, the then co-owners of the Radisson Hotel Mahipalpur, New Delhi, to allocate some land in one of their colonies in Gurgaon to establish the institute. They agreed as they had plans to grow their own hotel portfolio and would have a greater need for trained personnel. Later, I met with Jasminder Singh, the chairman and managing director of the Edwardian Group, UK, which had ten hotels in London under the Radisson brand. We had been meeting regularly at Radisson's annual business meetings and developed a mutual respect for each other. He liked my idea, and as it turned out, he was also contemplating philanthropic activities in India particularly in the field of education, and so he agreed to partner with us. A joint venture between Radisson Hotel International, USA, Radisson Edwardian UK, Unitech and Radisson Hotels Asia was set up.

We extensively researched potential collaborations with an overseas programme and shortlisted Johnson & Wales University, USA. Carlson had a very good relationship with the university and already had some kind of training tie-up with them for their US-based personnel. However, the deal for us didn't go through as the university required its students to physically attend their US campus in the last year but our concern was whether the majority of Indian students would get a visa at the requisite time – meaning, after three years of the programme in India, would they be able to get their degree? After much deliberation, we came to the conclusion that our concerns about their travel would remain and the experience would also be much more expensive for the students, which could dissuade them in the long run.

Facilitated by Jasminder Singh, we entered into a relationship with Oxford Brooks University (OBU) in the UK, which is the leading university for hotel management studies in the region, and where we felt a greater sense of connectivity Neelam took charge and connected with their liaison person, Grant Clendinning, who was a great support to us and serviced the deal as best as one can expect. We hired Dr Kamlesh Misra – who had similar experience running UK-based bachelor's of business administration and master's programmes – as director of the institute, and he helped to get other faculty, administrative executives and staff on board. Dr Vinnie Jauhari and Dr Venkatesh deserve a special mention for their contribution.

We first leased a building in Gurgaon that had an area of 20,000 square feet. We then arranged to refurbish the place according to the university's requirements. The first batches were admitted in the year 2000 in two undergraduate programmes – a Bachelor's of Science Honours degree in Hotel Management and the other in Business Studies. And so, the Institute for International Management and Technology (IIMT) was born.

Inspite of our success, funds were limited. We had exhausted most of the monies we had on building the required infrastructure for the delivery of the programme, which included a training kitchen facility, students' canteen and classroom furniture. Neelam and I took personal interest at every level and involved ourselves with the interiors to ensure that the design was not only functional but had a world-class look too. We were left with a small marketing budget. We could only afford to advertise for the seminars we held in various cities and often, Neelam and I would personally travel to make presentations for the programme in which we highlighted lucrative opportunities such as training overseas and luxe industry jobs. From inception, we received a great many applications and selected a qualified first batch of students.

The challenge then was to live up to the commitments we had made to students and parents on delivering an overseas experience. Although I was the managing director of the IIMT, Neelam was involved in every minute detail and took the entire responsibility along with me. When we travelled on work trips for Carlson or took vacations overseas, we made sure that we connected with people to arrange training positions for our students. From the first batch, we were successful in securing positions for each of our students either in the UK or US, and a few at the Ritz Carlton in Dubai. Soon these connections became the unique selling point for the institute and IIMT enjoyed a favourable reputation as being among the best hotel schools in the country. Since I was involved, we unofficially came to be known as the Carlson School for Hospitality. We slowly expanded our programme to include other business undergraduate and post-graduate courses, while we prioritized overall personality development in all respects, especially outside the classroom. Most students who graduated from IIMT found good jobs across the country as well as in UK. Some reached senior management positions, including becoming general managers, even overseas.

Even as all was going well, we had to receive approval from the All India Council for Technical Education (AICTE), which was mandatory. The AICTE put forth stringent requirements which, unfortunately, we did not have the funds to see through at the campus level. They also required the institute to be a non-profitable entity, owned by a trust, and IIMT did not fulfil either of these conditions. While efforts to apply for approval were in full swing, our partners from Unitech decided to divest from the company. In this partition, IIMT's ownership got transferred to the UMAK Trust, which belonged to Dr Ramesh Kapur and his family. We now had at least one of the requirements for approval. On becoming independent of Unitech, Dr Kapur inducted his children into his businesses. Amit Kapur, his younger son – an engineer himself with a post-graduate degree from Wharton School of Business in US – was given charge of their educational forays, which he wanted to nurture and scale up. It is at this stage that Neelam and I took a step back from our dream baby, which didn't need as much hand-holding as it was functioning well. I continued to be the managing director of IIMT for a few more years and in 2010, I handed over the reins to Amit Kapur.

However, both Neelam and I still bask in the glory of what our students of earlier batches have achieved. It is wonderful to see some of our students like Ankit Gaur, who is a very successful strategy consultant in London and some others who even became successful entrepreneurs in India and overseas.

Manav Joshi, who is the Group Food & Beverage director of the Edwardian Group of Hotels in London, overseeing Londoner and Mayfair Hotels amongst others. Many of the girl students from IIMT are excelling and are working at senior leadership positions. Recently I met the hotel manager of Oberoi Gurgaon, who happens to be an alumnus of the RHW hotel school (IIMT).

After Hubert Joly took over, the Carlson family decided to consolidate their businesses and do away with their joint venture associations, even in South Asia. They bought over most of these entities that had been formed over the years, and also merged RHW Management Services with the restructured Carlson entity in India. The new entity was called Carlson Hotels South Asia (CHSA). I was soon asked by then CEO of Carlson Companies, Hubert Joly to head the CHSA's activities in South Asia. Like J.B., Hubert Joly was a great supporter of the Asia-Pacific region and he too had developed a persuasive faith in me, for which I'm grateful. In a public debate at HICSA, he singularly credited me with the accelerated growth Carlson's companies experienced in India over other international chains. The CHSA set up a technical team headed by M.L. Bhattacharya to assist all Radisson and Park Plaza hotels under development by delivering advice at the concept stage and remaining involved till well after openings. The technical team provided comprehensive advice that ensured brand specifications were met with, while we ensured that the project was cost-effective for the owners.

It's important to highlight an interesting development in how strategic relationships worked in our region. The Bestech Group, led by Mr Dharmendra Bhandari and Mr Sunil Satija, who are real-estate developers, owned half an acre of land at a good location in Gurgaon. They approached me to help them build and operate a Great Kabab Factory (TGKF) restaurant on their site. On seeing the location I suggested they explore the possibility of building a hotel under our brand, which could include the restaurant. The idea appealed to them and they built a Park Plaza hotel, a brand which Carlson had recently acquired. The hotel had only forty-eight rooms but saw great success, so they were enthused to build another hotel, with thirty-two rooms, just 100 metres away. As a matter of policy the company didn't tie-up with hotels that had such a small room inventory. However, it was due to their unwavering commitment to develop three more hotels under our brands that the then president Jay Witzel, who was visiting India, noted the site's proximity to a Park Plaza hotel and allowed it to become a Radisson property. Bestech later went on to build Radisson Hotels in Noida, Indore and Nagpur and have also been our key ambassadors in the region. Given our relationship with them we formed a JV with Bestech aimed at growing Park Inn by Radisson and Radisson Red brands. This company has already signed nineteen hotels, is scheduled to develop thirty more, and has commissioned our first Radisson Red hotel in Mohali, Chandigarh, whose new concept has been well-received by the market. We are also proud of our other strategic partners like GRT Hotels, MBD, Concord Hospitality, AB Hotels and DS Group who stood by us in our formative years. Our focus on establishing strategic relationships continues. One of our great ambassador was Gautam Kapoor, owner of Radisson Hotel Jallander. This hotel established our forey in tier 2 towns in India. A few years back we closed on a major deal with Mushtaq Chaya Group in J&K, which has already delivered five operational hotels, three more under development in just 3-4 years.

After a steady series of mergers and takeovers, the Carlson family sold their hospitality business to HNA, an investment group. HNA further sold the business to Jing Jiang, who are the current owners. Jing Jiang already has a mammoth presence in Asia Pacific, parts of Europe, and USA. The Carlson Hospitality Group was then renamed as the Radisson Hotel Group. To retain the Radisson name was a poignant decision as the brand has gained worldwide recognition and is a preferred destination in the upper upscale and most recently in luxury segment.

More recently in 2017, Federico González – who had taken over as president and CEO of the Radisson Hotel Group – visited India. The company was formulating its five-year plan and he actively involved me in developing strategies going forward, and I was honoured by the responsibility. Fede, as he is affectionately called, is highly structured, focused and loves to challenge his team. The growth targets we fixed were difficult but attainable. Since then, I have been chairman emeritus and principal advisor to the Radisson Hotel Group, South Asia. As my designation suggests, my main focus is to help the company in its growth, overall positioning, manage relationships with our owners and offer advice whenever needed. We have a great team in India headed by Zubin Saxena and have collectively been able to widely pursue RHG's growth. I also serve on RHG's related boards in India. It gives me immense satisfaction to share that even in the exceptionally difficult times of Covid-19 pandemic, and the tough competition facing industries across a spectrum, I have personally been involved in facilitating the development and signing of at least 50 per cent of deals in the last five years.

Today the Radisson Hotel Group has been a market leader of sorts. We have been the largest international hotel chain in the region until the merger of Starwood and Marriott took place in 2020. The secret of our accelerated growth story is that from the outset, we identified sites and hotel developers in tier-2 and tier-3 cities, where other brands had no presence and no strategic inclination to enter. Today RHG has fourteen hotels in just the state of Punjab. Surely one of the major handicaps in our developmental activities in South Asia has been that the company never made any investment in real estate, until the joint venture with Bestech Hospitality to establish our latest brand – Radisson Red – was formed. Had we seeded the market along the way, we likely would have doubled our portfolio.

Having said that, we are proud to be amongst the largest hotel groups in India. It has been most gratifying to be in a position of overseeing franchising managing assets worth over $ 1.5 billion and to see Radisson's expeditious growth over the years.

VI

Food and Beverage Projects

A menu of ideas and a chef's will to experiment

I have always been keen to experiment with ideas in the food and beverage (F&B) sector, particularly after I attended several programmes at the Hotelfachschule, Hamburg, as well as courses conducted by Cornell University, USA. Although I had trained mostly in the front office, my first posting as assistant manager, F&B was at Jammu Ashok. I underwent a quick training programme especially formulated for me at Akbar Hotel, New Delhi, where I trained at the Indian restaurant Sheesh Mahal and at the coffee shop Madhuban. Both these outlets were known for their food and were popular with Delhiites, as well as people visiting from other cities and international guests. I also spent time training in the kitchen under chef Om Prakash, who was formally the head cook at famous restaurants Kake-Da-Hotel and National which are famous for tandoori chicken and butter chicken. Chef Om Prakash was handicapped and cooked only with one hand and although he was the ex sous chef at Akbar hotel, he cooked food with an unfiltered passion. Among other things he introduced paneer pasanda, which was a top-selling item on the menu. At the same time, ITDC had hired experts from Steigenberger Hotels, West Germany, to assist in packaging and presentation of our food and beverage offerings at Akbar and Ashok hotels. The experts looked into small things like crockery, cutlery, napery and presentation of each dish. I learned a great deal from them, and it was very exciting to have an opportunity to become quickly exposed to international standards. It is at this time that my fascination for the sector began. Later, during my various travels overseas, I made it a point to visit all the famous eateries, even at my own expense, and take ideas from these experiences. I would especially take photographs of plating and presentation examples and ask my team to try to emulate some of these takeaways.

I also participated in various food festivals as the head of cultural delegations in most parts of the world, which gave me ample exposure to the latest trends in the culinary arts. Since I've frequently had the opportunity to manage smaller scale hotels, I've been able to execute all sorts of ideas and adapt my applications to market changes. With a steep learning curve, I remained hugely encouraged to ideate and implement both intrapreneurial and entrepreneurial projects throughout my career.

When I had just become the general manager at the Ashok Hotel, New Delhi, one of my immediate priorities was to revamp our F&B offerings. I had a great team to work with, consisting of Roger Moncourt, a French gentleman who was the corporate executive chef, Chef Fernandes, S.B. Subbarwal, RM and B.P. Singh, who served as the F&B manager of the hotel. Together we launched Burgundy, a formal dining, French cuisine restaurant; Frontier, a semi-casual, Northwest Frontier Indian food restaurant; China Town, for Chinese cuisine; and the Garden Bar, which was conceptualized with international interiors. We had lined up the openings of our culinary cohort for the same day, to be aligned with the Non-aligned Meeting, which occurred at the hotel in the early 1980s. Each restaurant was driven by a commitment to authenticity and style. Chef Moncourt even went to the extent of growing a herb garden in the hotel's backyard, as much of what he required for French cuisine were not easily available in Indian markets in those days. For Frontier, we did a lot of research and development to unearth ancient recipes from Rampur, Varanasi and Lucknow in Uttar Pradesh and the cuisines of the Mughal Era and North West Frontier, now a part of Pakistan. Ideas were also borrowed from Turkish and Middle Eastern kababs. The chefs invented several new kabab recipes that were not known to the market, such as bannu kabab, Shahjahani kabab etc. They offered a reintroduction of traditional recipes (sometimes with a twist) to discerning customers. Most Chinese restaurants in countries served only Cantonese food while Szechuan food was gaining popularity worldwide, but because we lacked the right resources, we outsourced its operations. The hotel also had a Japanese restaurant called Tokyo, the first of its kind in Delhi, which helped us to draw in a lot of Japanese clientele, including the Suzuki team, who were setting up their plant in Haryana and business in India. Tokyo was set up in collaboration with Japan Airlines. While conceptualizing the restaurant, I was part of the team that visited Japan to experience and understand traditional Japanese food and restaurant operations. I recall that we were invited by the CEO of Japan Airlines to a very famous and expensive restaurant in Tokyo. We were served items like monkey head. The very names put us Indians off trying the dishes and we barely ate anything. Nevertheless, the experience helped us to ascertain that such cuisine would not be acceptable to the Indian palate or psyche. So we researched, sought out and tasted many other branches and dishes of Japanese cuisine and formulated our menu accordingly, keeping the Indian market in mind. Domestic market for Japanese food continues to grow but the menu is largely structured to its acceptability locally. Puneet Chhatwal excelled in launching "TOKYO", our first Japanese restaurant in the region.

In a short time, all our culinary concepts became very popular not only with hotel residents but also local clientele, who regularly frequented and patronized us. It is worthy of note that all these restaurants were run by young managers in their early twenties, which was unheard of in the industry in 1982. Many of these managers have become industry leaders today. The success of these restaurants helped us to position the hotel more highly and also fill our rooms, which were newly renovated. Our F&B revamp led to the hotel becoming a preferred venue for accommodation and gave a big boost to our conference and wedding business.

A unique undertaking for a five-star hotel in the public sector like the Ashok was the setting up of Chaupal, a restaurant at the behest the then tourism minister of India, who wanted to initiate a village-themed restaurant acting as a guardian for rural India. When translated into the English, *chaupal* refers to a public place for meetings in a village and is typically an outdoor venue. Inspired by its cultural symbolism in rural Indian lifestyle, we created an outdoor restaurant where we used *charpai*s, or strung jute beds, as furniture and complemented it with rustic décor. The food was served in baked clay, brass and leaf plates and bowls, as a prevalent custom in rural homes. Chopal represented a mélange of elevated rural sensibility, which spoke well to the public sector as much as juxtaposition in that despite being in a five-star hotel, the restaurant offered no luxury. As a place of novelty, we received many curious visitors. Unfortunately, over time the sales were insufficient for us to continue operations, and we soon had to shut the restaurant.

In the mid 1980s, the USSR was still an integrated country and the iron curtain had not yet been lifted. The governments of the USSR and India were keen to work together to boost overall trade and tourism between the two countries. In order to kickstart the process, both governments initially focused on promoting Indian cuisine and culture. As a result of this, we were entrusted with the very first joint venture ever created by the USSR with India – which led to a year-long festival celebrating their respective cultures in the other country. I was fortunate to be involved in both these festivals in as far as the showcasing of food and handling accommodation was concerned. Coincidentally my wife Neelam was invited to coordinate the logistics by ministry of culture Government of India for the USSR festival in India and also the closing ceremony of the Indian festival in Moscow. Both of us have had the privilege of meeting the cultural tsars and celebrities in the Soviet Union, some of whom even became our friends, including members of the Bolshoi ballet group and orchestra troupe.

In spite of a host of breathtakingly beautiful architectural buildings – the remnants of a capitalistic past – the capital city of Moscow had little to no standalone restaurants outside of a few hotels and public institutions. Dining out was yet to develop as a social concept. One of the very first agreements, in May 1985, between President Gorbachev and Prime Minister Rajiv Gandhi was the formulation of a joint venture in Moscow to promote Indian food and culture. As general manager at the Ashok Hotel, I was entrusted the responsibility of concluding this tie-up and operationalizing these two restaurants. My colleague O.N. Verma and I visited Moscow several times, sometimes staying there for weeks together, where we met with our Soviet counterparts to discuss the structure and commissioning of the units.

During our first visit, on arrival in Moscow we were picked up in a large limousine that hurtled down the wide middle lane on the roads. I later learned that it was a privilege to drive in the middle lane, available to only the politburo – or the policymaking committee of the communist party – and their select few guests. We were put up at a *dacha* – a seasonal or second home outside the city of Moscow. The house rested on acres of land in an isolated area, with meagre furnishings and no semblance of comfort. So we requested to be accommodated at a hotel instead, and the authorities very kindly agreed. They moved us to the thirty storey Rossiya Hotel in the heart of Moscow, with 7500 beds. It was briefly known as the largest hotel in the world, and is now referred to as one of the seven sisters in Russia. I had considered the Ashok Hotel in Delhi to be an enormous construction, but I had to reconsider my perception on seeing Rossiya Hotel. However, the hotel was unique, in that its size did not imply grandeur. The rooms that were allotted to us were not more than 100 square feet each. The only amenity in the bathroom, besides a thin huckaback towel, was a used soap. When I asked housekeeping for a fresh soap, she said, 'Only one person has used it before you.' Though there were some hotels that were upscale and commanded a rate of over USD 600 per night, our experience largely reflected the level of hospitality prevalent in the industry in Moscow at that time.

We undertook rounds of discussion and negotiations with the mayor of Moscow and his team as we worked to set up the Moscow–Ashok Corporation that would oversee the operations of the two proposed Indian restaurants in Moscow. Each time we appeared to reach an accord, talks would break down at the last minute. Some of their junior officers wanted to retain control particularly in the procurement process while we wanted a free hand. The discussions went on for a few weeks. One time Mr Verma and I got so frustrated that we said in Hindi: '*Yeh samaj nahi sakte hain – kya karre!*' (They can't understand what to do!) To our horror, one of them retorted, '*Hum gadhe nahi hain!*' (We are not donkeys!) We all laughed. They were so sporting about it that instead of being a deal-breaker, we had wound up with an ice-breaker. We finally signed the deal for 'The Delhi' restaurants.

Both locations of 'The Delhi' were designed by Sarbjit Singh – now the principal designer at Fab Interiors – with interiors that were typical of Indian cuisine restaurants in India, using key Indian materials like stone-work, paintings and other artifacts. Some of the furniture was also designed to create a typical Indian ambience but with an elevated feel. One of the restaurants was conceived for foreigners who would spend money in dollars, and the other was meant for local residents who would be paying in roubles. Those days foreign exchange, particularly dollars, was highly coveted and the Soviet enterprise wanted to earn in dollars by attracting diplomats from different embassies. The guest who paid in dollars also received privileged service and amenities. The project took about six months to complete. We established a central kitchen, and offered the same menu at both restaurants.

At first the restaurants were open only for dinner, but with a raging popularity among locals and diplomats, people started queuing up in the middle of the afternoon. Daily sales crossed the total sales of all of ITDC's restaurants in India at the time – a success that was not only exhilarating but baffling as well.

We selected a team from ITDC's best resources to be posted in Moscow to operate the outlets. However, I was given to understand that almost all the team members were apprehensive about relocating to the USSR, although a Superpower, since they didn't know what to expect from a communist country. Although India was socialistic, it was still democratic. In their very first week in Moscow, our Indian management team consisting of Shishir Saxena and Rajiv Makin and their team were in a meeting with Mrs Krugalaya, chairperson of the Moscow–Ashok Corporation. She said to Rajiv, 'You (Indians) come from a very advanced country, and you have to teach our people (Russians) how to manage a good quality restaurant.' Her comment inspired a much-needed confidence boost in the team.

When we newly opened the restaurants, we had an executive chef from ITDC – Mr Atul Gokhale – as well as a Russian chef to come together to manage the kitchens. The recipes we handed out had precise measurements to standardize the dishes we would serve. The Russian chef would weigh each dish and approve its mensurements before handing it over to a waiter. However, he ran into constant trouble when someone ordered a *seekh* kabab, which is made out of minced meat. Since it is rolled by hand, it wasn't always possible to maintain the exact weight each time. The Indian chef tried to explain this to his Russian colleague that chopping any excess portion wouldn't help – but to no avail. We certainly experienced such cultural miscommunications as is perhaps expected from such a situation. In a joint meeting between the Indian and Russian management teams Mr Achal Malhotra – a counsellor at the Indian embassy and a coordinator for the joint venture overseeing the restaurants – indicated that since the restaurant was Indian, the Indian management would be given a final say over the Russians. He indirectly suggested that in case of further problems, the Indian embassy would inform Mr Gorbachev, the then President of the USSR about their non-cooperation.

Mr Yelstin, who was the deputate of the Krasnaya Polyana district in Moscow, where the Delhi Restaurant was located, visited once. Due to security reasons, he visited around 4 p.m. in the afternoon. He was received by Rajiv Makin and Mrs Krugalaya and taken around the restaurant. A special menu was prepared and served to him in what was probably a first savoury encounter with Indian cuisine. Rajiv informed him that all the raw material used in the restaurant was brought from India, except the linen and cutlery. To this, Mr Yelstin commented, 'Why did you procure these things from here? Even these should have been brought from India, since Indian linen and cutlery are of very good quality.' Such comments made Rajiv and his team proud to be Indians and back at the corporate office in Delhi, we were also happy to hear this feedback. Mr Yeltsin later became the President of the USSR and visited the Delhi restaurant many times as a great ambassador of Indian cuisine.

Due to the popularity and success of our joint venture restaurant, Indo-Soviet bilateral partnership also received a big boost. Immediately after opening, an Indo-Soviet joint feature film was made and shot primarily in the USSR. The film was titled *Ajooba* in Hindi and *The Black Prince* in English. The main cast included big Bollywood stars like Amitabh Bachchan and Shashi Kapoor.

Since Delhi restaurant was considered the best as it served authentic Indian food in an Indian ambience, all VIPs including Indian delegations, embassy parties and even film-stars were regular guests. To provide entertainment, the Rouble Hall had a Russian band play to a vibrant and usually packed dance floor. The band even learned a few Hindi songs which they sang to perfection. A popular number at the time was: '*Goron ki na kalon ki, duniya hai dil walon ki*'. The other hall, created for foreigners, organized Indian classical dance performances like Kathak and Bharatnatyam, whose traditional choreographies were executed beautifully by Russian artistes.

Once Bollywood actor Shashi Kapoor came to the restaurant for dinner. As he was readying to leave after his meal, the band began performing an Indian song and the famous actor stood by the gate to hear it till its end. He clapped loudly, with a drink still in his hand. The security guard became alerted to a guest carrying a glass out of the restaurant and informed the manager, who informed him that this guest was none other than Raj Kapoor's younger brother. The security guard then encouraged Shashi Kapoor to take his drink along with him, such was the respect Russians had for Raj Kapoor and the intimacy with which they appreciated Bollywood.

The Delhi restaurant was considered to be the best in Moscow for decades. We were then invited by the Government of Estonia in Tallin as well as in Helsinki, Finland, to open more joint ventures with their governments. Though initial visits and discussions did take place, somehow the deal could not be finalized because the Government of USSR was not very clear about their own policies post the fall of the communist regime. However, this exposure gave us the opportunity to set up similar restaurants in Prague (in then Czechoslovakia) and Yugoslavia (which never opened), and much later we established a successful restaurant in New Zealand too.

In spite of years of experience with restaurants, working in the food and beverage industry in the helm of the private sector was a different experience altogether. During my tenure in Singapore working with the Carlson Hospitality Group, Radisson Hotels Asia was entrusted with responsibility of promoting the franchising of the world-loved TGI Fridays in the ASEAN countries and South East Asia. TGIF, a popular short-hand for the restaurant, was initially conceived by a private entrepreneur named Alan Stillman in New York in 1965. The Carlson family bought the rights to develop and franchise TGIF in 1975, when the brand had just twelve restaurants. The brand grew to over 900 restaurants in operation in sixty countries. CNBC quotes that Carlson sold off the brand in 2013 for USD 800 million.

As I shared previously, Rajan and I knew Tunku Iskander, owner of the Melawar Group and previously president of the Pacific Area Travel Association (PATA). We approached him with the idea for opening a franchise in Singapore and were successful in forming a joint venture with his company. We went on to open multiple outlets in the region, with the first TGI Fridays in a standalone glass house attached to the Park Mall on Orchard Road – a landmark location. From its introduction to the Asian market, the restaurant was an unforgettable success. I was a director on the board and also involved in operations from time to time.

Rajan then introduced me to B.S. Ong, the chairman of HPL Properties, Singapore, who owned the Concord Hotel Group, the Hilton Hotel on Orchard Road, the Four Seasons Hotel and the Meridien Hotel in Singapore, among others. We signed a master franchise for TGI Fridays with him for Japan, however these opened much later due to limited key locations and high rentals.

The current rights to develop Fridays in Asia-Pacific are with Universal Success, a company owned by an ex colleague Prasoon Mukerjee.

With his company Indo-Pacific, Rajan also invested in and opened an upscale Indian venue called the Royal Bengal Restaurant in Boat Quay, a popular gastronomical neighbourhood in Singapore. I was involved in setting it up as well as its governance. The restaurant was inaugurated by the

President of Singapore. With the success of its launch, Rajan became enthusiastic about increasing scale of investment in F&B concepts. We then opened a Goan restaurant in Holland Village called Casa de Goa. Both restaurants drew in great business while we were local residents.

The opening ceremony of the Boutique – Royal Bengal restaurant was limited to some very important leaders, bureaucrats and business tycoons of Singapore. Amongst them was Lee Hsien Loong, popularly known as B.G. Lee. In those days he was brigadier general. Rajan hosted the President of Singapore at his table and Neelam & I were hosting B.G. Lee and his wife. We had a very interesting evening with them and learnt a lesson or two on humility and discipline. Although he was the son of Lee Kuan Yew, the then Prime Minister of the country, he was extremely unassuming. He carried a pager instead of a mobile phone. Although mobile phones had already been introduced in Singapore, but he still opted to use the pager, like any commoner. During our conversation we also learnt that they didn't install a television for the children, who were allowed to watch TV under guidance of their grandfather only. Not only were we impressed beyond words but also learnt how important it is to nurture the right values in children and always remain grounded.

Rajan sold off the restaurants when we moved back to India, with the concern that we would not be able to manage operations well from such a distance. Another reason was the stringent visa rules prevalent in Singapore. Once, when the Singaporean visas for two of our Indian chefs expired, the administrator in-charge of reapplication forgot to do so. In effect, their working without permits was considered a breach of law. Being directors, Rajan and I had to bear responsibility. The two chefs were held in lock-up through no fault of their own. It was with great difficulty that we were able to prove that we had not retained them deliberately. We managed their release and put them on a flight back to India.

Another interesting project in which I had the opportunity to partner with Biki Oberoi, Chairman Oberoi hotels, B.S Ong, chairman, HPL, Singapore and Rajan Jetley to create and establish an Indian Quick Service Restaurant brand and grow it worldwide. Adequate funds were infused into building the concept that were visualised by the stakeholders. We had several meetings in Singapore, Delhi and even London, which included extensive R&D and numerous food tasting rounds to build an acceptable and sustainable concept.

We even collaborated with the Singapore Government agencies like Shatec, (Singapore Tourism & hotel school). Temasek, a global investment company based in Singapore, expressed its willingness to participate and lead the funding.

Chef Richard Graham was assigned the task of undertaking the menu development. The initial reaction to food trials was very positive and all of us felt that the product would be highly acceptable globally.

Because of the appreciation for Indian cuisine by the British, we decided to open the first restaurant in London. We shortlisted a location on Bond Street, close to Oxford Street. I was stationed in London for sometime, and since Biki Oberoi spent substantial time in London those days, we often held meetings at his home.

One day during one of our meetings on finalising the service style an issue arose on its positioning and its differentiation. Unfortunately, there was a difference of opinion as to whether to position it as casual dinning concept or a QSR. As a result of this disagreement the project was unfortunately shelved.

This has been one of my major regrets in life.

I still believe that the concept that we had conceptualized would've been a roaring success and none till now has introduced an Indian QSR concept of that kind.

In 1996, when the F&B offerings of the Radisson Hotel Delhi, Mahipalpur, were being planned, general manager and vice president Sanjiv Tyagi conceived the idea of naming the

Indian food restaurant 'The Great Kabab Factory'. At that time, one might have thought such a claim was like 'putting the cart before the horse'. But we ran with it. The interior designer designed interiors befitting its name and the menu and service style were also planned accordingly.

Sanjiv oversaw the development of this unique concept. *Galouti*, the signature kabab, was a speciality of the Tunda family of Lucknow, and it is the family who trained the hotel staff. The word *galouti* translates to a 'thing that melts in the mouth'. The term first originated in the eighteenth century kitchens of Lucknow's Nawab Asad-ud-Daula, who was extremely fond of kababs, from the Turkish kitchens then brought to India by the Afghans and later popularized by the Mughals. It was enjoyed for breakfast with naan in the thirteenth century. At the Great Kabab Factory, special recipes were developed for each kabab, which were put through rigorous food tasting sessions till the recipes were perfected and approved. Once the concept was ready, a variety of people from all walks of life, including food critics like Jiggs Kalra, fashion designers Rina Dhaka and J.J. Vallaya and other influencers, were invited to comment on the food and style of service. With their inputs, a unique service style was born. For the first time, a buffet was presented at the table by servers. We now had a homegrown concept. Seeing its roaring success, I decided to trademark the brand and franchise the concept and personally helped develop the concept into a franchise model. Rajeev Chowdhary, the executive chef, needs special mention for the quality of food, which was later replicated in all the Great Kabab Factory restaurants. Ashna Kapur, director, UMAK, now personally oversees the growth and successful operation of TGKF.

The food and beverage industry in India is becoming more and more profitable each year. It makes up around 3 per cent of

India's GDP. Food is a necessity as much as a luxury, and it is one of those things that can never really fall out of trend.

Along with the population boom in India, the demand for ready-to-eat food is also growing. More and more families are becoming nuclear and both spouses are working out of the house. While this enhances their ability to spend, it also leaves them little time to do household chores like cooking. With this increase in middle-class income, consumer needs and trends are also changing. The industry today provides plenty of scope for innovation, personalization and premiumization in food concepts. However, consumers are also becoming more and more discerning and knowledgeable because of increased exposure due to travel. So they want authentic food and are ever-ready to try new concepts and fusion cuisines. Thus, there has been a shift in consumption habits of Indian consumers from traditional food flavours to global and fusion food. This has given a big boost to the gourmet food market in India, which is currently over USD 1.3 billion.

However, I believe only those restaurant concepts that can adapt to changing demands will survive and grow too. With innovation comes more opportunities to grow and also expand into new markets, all while maintaining a competitive advantage. Along with food, the beverage industry has also grown exponentially and will continue to see upward swing in the years to come. Bartenders who create and churn out exciting new cocktails are much in spotlight, altering the outlook on bartending to a lucrative, passion-driven and respected profession. It is believed that the average net profit of a successful bar is more than the average annual return from the stock market, so it is considered a good business, provided one doesn't over-invest in real estate, lease money or interiors. In India too, chef-owned restaurants are becoming popular just like in Western countries, and one can find many such special joints in cities like Delhi, Mumbai and Goa. I am told approximately 20 per cent of chefs are now turning into entrepreneurs.

All in all, a career in F&B can be very rewarding. One can pursue a plethora of opportunities – from becoming an executive or corporate chef and starting one's own restaurant in the business to opening a chain of restaurants and taking up big contracts in corporate offices, cloud kitchens or airline catering. Starting one's own culinary academy, food packaging or delivery business are potential options too. In the service area, one can aspire to be the director of F&B or a director of banquets. These jobs often lead to the position of general manager as one grows in experience.

Food touches everyone's life in some form or the other, be it a wedding, a social gathering, a small get-together or even a private bereavement or indulgence. Hence, there is an immense scope of growth and opportunities for small to big investors and entrepreneurs in the food and beverage business. The number of users in the F&B market is estimated to reach 346.9 million by 2025.

VII

Mentors and Fostering Young Talent

A mutual relationship is worth its weight in gold

I've been fortunate to find the right mentor at every stage of my life. When I was young, my parents were my moral anchors and life teachers. They valued understanding and perspective, and encouraged me to put myself in another's shoes before making a judgement. They also taught me the importance of being satisfied with less, helping others in their time of need and staying humble.

I've carried these teachings with me throughout my life. When I started moving on up I realized I needed to develop my own vision and grow my standards. Regarding the latter, though affordability posed an issue for me for many years, I was accustomed to living within my means. But I realized growth could be experienced in various ways, and refining one's mindset is a worthier goal than focusing on material life. Truthfully, in my experience, growth will always yield more growth.

If I had to summarize the key takeaways from my mentors, it would be to focus on my strengths and to not worry so much about things I wasn't good at. I also learned to trade in shyness and ask for help when I needed it, which inculcated such a positive attitude that it enabled me to be more effective. A good mentor should be able to make their mentee assess themselves correctly and recognize where they feel the need for improvement, and then help them build a road-map to that future.

It is indeed a gift to find the right mentor at the right time in your life. I am lucky to have been guided by reverent role models, like Psyche Nigam, who advised me to accept my first posting in Jammu, and senior colleagues like O.N. Verma and N.N. Khetrapal, who guided me to focus on people management and finance in my early days. I am also grateful to have had the opportunity to pay it forward, as they say, to my own mentees, keeping in mind the tenets of good mentorship that I was most fortunate to experience myself as well. Here I dedicate a heartfelt thanks to both my mentors and mentees.

J.P. Sharma

My first mentor in this industry was Mr J.P. Sharma, the principal at IHM Pusa. He taught me the importance and manners of maintaining relationships with the industry and media when I was the president of the Students Association. He was very fond of both Neelam and me and we're grateful to him for the affection and confidence he inculcated in us. This head-start to leadership has held me in good stead throughout my working career.

S.K. Misra

Mr Misra, a boss I most respect, took over as chairman and managing director of ITDC. We all knew him as the great bureaucrat from Haryana who had changed the face of the India's tourism. We were all in awe of his aristocratic personality. He was known as 'Suspension Kumar'. He belled the cat, so to say, soon after taking over the company. Anyone who did not deliver on the job or made a deliberate mistake was immediately suspended.

Mr Misra taught me the importance of being a visionary to achieve greater heights. He was a firm administrator and from him I learned to call a spade a spade, to pre-empt and plan in advance and then work towards my objectives. He was a man of few words with the resilience to revise even his own decisions, which encouraged me never to shy away from changing my mind for the greater good. His confidence in me inspired the learning that support for one's subordinates and colleagues can have a great effect not only on an individual's career but also the company's future. Because of Mr Misra's faith in me, he sent me on various missions overseas to represent the country or the company on several occasions.

In my later years I became the head of the Ashok Group of Hotels, while Devi Lal was the deputy prime minister and also held the portfolio of tourism. Even when Devi Lal and I had disagreements on various issues, it was only Mr Misra who stood by me even at the cost of his own relationship with the deputy prime minister. Once someone became a friend of Mr Misra's, he would remain a friend forever.

Rajan Jetley

As I've shared, I first met Rajan Jetley when he joined India Tourism Development Corporation (ITDC) as managing director in 1982. After his taking over, he came to the Samrat project office and Neelam – who was the designated executive housekeeper – walked in to put a file on my table, and met with him instead. Later I understood that Rajan was perplexed to find my wife instead of me in my office. I do not think he went away with positive feelings about us – a husband-wife operation. However, he must have been briefed by his corporate team on our professional backgrounds and there was no resentment thereafter.

Rajan got immediately involved in the planning of ITDC's contemporary face-lift, so we would meet frequently. These interactions likely gave him a better understanding of my capabilities and dedication. It is Rajan who entrusted me with the responsibility of becoming the youngest ever general manager of the company's flagship enterprise – the Ashok Hotel, with 586 rooms. After the very successful run at the Ashok Hotel, Rajan promoted me to vice president and gave me an opportunity to become involved with other facets of ITDC's businesses. I soon saw myself as Rajan's Officer on Special Duty (OSD). Through this position, I was now involved in all the business verticals of ITDC. I was party to all policymaking and operational decisions for each business vertical, including travel, transport, publicity and printing, which did a lot of work for the Ministry of Tourism and state governments.

I learned so much from observing Rajan's handling of ITDC's businesses and how adeptly he dealt with the demands of politicians and bureaucrats alike. I am privy to a decision that he took in the interest of the company when Mr H.K.L. Bhagat, the then tourism minister, called him to reverse one of his decisions. Rajan politely yet firmly told him that his decision would prevail since he was the managing director and so the accountability of the decision lay with him too. Working with and for him, I gained experience in matters far beyond the horizon of hotel operations.

Rajan was a strong administrator but always remained supportive to his team. Although he was mostly rational and clear-headed, he could sometimes be difficult. As his OSD I held a position of trust, and the onus was on me to ensure that no issues arose. Most of the time I was successful, but there were moments he was determined to have his way, which if executed, could have had serious consequences. In such situations I would step back, give us some time, even meet over a drink, then broach the subject in a more relaxed atmosphere and attempt to reason out what would be right.

In 1987, Rajan left ITDC and moved to Mumbai to become the MD & CEO of Air India. By then we had developed mutual respect and faith in each other and continued to lend any kind of help and support. In the meantime, I had moved on up to become the head of the hotels division of the group. From Air India, Rajan moved to Singapore to work for Nabisco. We kept in touch, and we would also meet on his trips to Delhi.

I am indebted to Rajan to have supported me in my early years in Singapore, without which I could not have forged ahead in my career. It is his tutelage that groomed me to not only head a large corporation, but also become an entrepreneur.

B.K. Goswami

I was first introduced to Mr Billoo Goswami, as he was popularly known, when he was commissioner of Meerut division in Uttar Pradesh in the early eighties. When he became chief secretary of Jammu & Kashmir, he asked me to contribute towards the state since I hailed from there. It is at his behest that we set up the restaurant Jaikara, which catered to over 30,000 daily pilgrims visiting the Mata Vaishno Devi Shrine. Our relationship was consolidated when he became director general of tourism for the Government of India and also had the additional charge as acting chairman of ITDC. He urged me to contribute more towards the development of tourism in various states, particularly Uttar Pradesh, Madhya Pradesh, Jammu & Kashmir and West Bengal. He was instrumental in getting me nominated on several state tourism boards, which also led to nominations on tourism- and travel-related bodies in India and Asia such as PATA. Even after I started business development for Carlson Hotels, Mr Goswami remained instrumental in introducing me to prominent businessmen and many international investors with whom we built hotels in various places.

Mr Goswami taught me how to enhance my vision and role from being a hotelier to becoming a tourism professional as well. From my association with him, I began to better understand that the hospitality industry was an integral part of travel and tourism industry. They are inter-dependent and need one another's support at all times, especially in terms of infrastructural growth. He taught me to take an umbrella view and ensure that all our verticals operate in a collaborative manner. He continues to extend his support to me.

Juergen Bartels

If it had not been for Juergen Bartels, I would not have had the opportunity to work with Carlson Hotels. It was J.B. who identified me for the development role for Radisson Hotels in Asia. He often treated me like a younger brother and every time we met, he would say to me: 'K.B., I want to see you as a millionaire.' Until I met J.B., I was a conservative person but he taught me to dream big, nurture objectives that may feel unachievable at the outset, and to never give up. His attitude and big heart were the encouragement I needed to explore the unknown territories of tier-2 and tier-3 markets in India. He leads a retired life now and we are still in touch.

Jim Olson

Jim Olson was the VP of development for Radisson Hotels Worldwide and specifically in charge of development in the Asia-Pacific for all Carlson brands. I first met him in Singapore and we took an immediate liking to each other. From my interactions with him I knew, besides being a perfect gentleman, he was also very knowledgeable and thorough at his job. Jim visited the region periodically and we often travelled together to pursue development opportunities in many unknown territories.

It is Jim who taught me the entire gamut of development work. Until then, I had been an operations person. He was sensitive to each culture and astutely realized that we could not change the world in many respects. In cases that involved cultural issues, he encouraged us to change our strategy to what would be more accepted in that country or region. Not only did I learn negotiation skills from him, but also learned to feel confidence in the work I had undertaken.

He guided me through many years of our association, and we became a kind of duo, a team. Our companionship helped me deliver on Carlson's expectations and commitments and had he lived a longer life, he would have enjoyed the fruits of the foundation that he had so well laid out.

Whenever I visited Minneapolis, Jim would invite all of us to his home. Jacque, his lovely wife, would prepare food, especially a fish that I liked. The warmth of their hospitality and love will remain in our thoughts forever. Unfortunately, we lost Jim very early at the age of fifty-six. His passing came as a shock to all of us, and besides my wife and I, my son Amit was also in grief and mourned his death equally. Jim and Jacque had been his family in Minnesota in the days when he was newly married and had moved to Minneapolis. Jim would take Amit and Bhavna, our daughter in-law, out for a meal on their birthdays and anniversaries, filling in for us, as we were living in India. We had the solace that our children were not alone in a far-off country, especially in their early years, when Amit's job paid him a meagre salary and there were very few Indian families living there, as compared to now. We had the comfort of knowing their Minnesota Mom and Dad would take care of their needs if there was an emergency.

Over this period we gained mutual respect for each other, and a kind of unsaid friendship grew. I say this because I had considered him to be my mentor and boss, but whenever we were not at work, he would behave just like a friend. I was initially afraid to cross the line and remained in the realm of our business relationship. It is Jim who taught me how to manage the boundaries between work and friendship.

To honour Jim's contributions to the growth of Carlson Hotels in India, we re-christened the IIMT (hotel school) library and named it the Jim Olson Library. I also dedicated my Carlson Fellowship Award in Jim's honour and invited Jacque Olson to not only be present at the ceremony held at the Radisson in downtown Minneapolis but also receive the award with me.

Fostering Young Talent

In the early 1980s, when I became the general manager of ITDC's airport hotel in Kolkata, I was already nurturing young executives to develop their managerial skills. It is also my nature to help people for a genuine cause. As they say, sometimes it is in giving that one receives, and I was lucky to come by a team that helped me establish my own stead in the early years.

I remember an instance, when I had just taken over as GM, my secretary informed me that a young man, then unknown to any of us, wanted to meet me. Despite not knowing the person, I agreed to meet him and patiently heard his story. He informed me that he had been selected by ITDC as a management trainee and was asked to report immediately to New Delhi. But he couldn't go to Delhi right away as his mother had passed away only two days prior, and he needed to be present in Kolkata for ten more days or so to perform the religious rites. ITDC's personnel department had turned down his request to allow him to join ten days later and instead said that if he didn't join on the stipulated date, their offer would stand withdrawn. Realizing there could be serious consequences to his career, which was still to begin, I felt the urge to come to his rescue. Since processes at headquarters had clearly overtaken an emotional quotient, I decided to give him a chance and took a very unconventional decision. Without prior permission, I asked him to join ITDC's Kolkata hotel instead and granted him leave for the required number of days. Luckily my actions were approved on humanitarian grounds. This gentleman is no other than **Prasoon Mukerjee**, chairman and managing director of Universal Success, who has not only excelled professionally as a businessmen but is also among the wealthiest Indian entrepreneurs in South Asia. I am so happy that he has now acquired rights for developing Fridays' in the entire Asia-Pacific region. He represents and leads Singapore government business associations globally.

I am privileged, that despite his phenomenal achievements in Busines in Asia, he not only considers me part of the family but treats me with immense respect and concern. He makes a point to call almost every week. At his son's marriage reception in Singapore, he had invited only few select including the chairman of Tata Group of companies, me and a very senior politician to be seated on the top table along with the bride, bride groom and the parents.

As a young GM of the Ashok Hotel, I was lucky to get a team of highly talented, motivated and committed young individuals. While I may have been directly or indirectly instrumental in honing their talent and ensuring their growth within the organization, I definitely owe my own success as general manager to each of them. Prominent among them are **Puneet Chhatwal**, who worked as the first manager of Tokyo – the newly opened Japanese restaurant at the Ashok Hotel. He left for Paris to do an MBA and later joined the Carlson Rezidor Hotel Group, where he quickly moved up the ladder to head the company's development in Europe, the Middle East and Africa. Carlson's growth in these regions is greatly attributed to his efforts in executing Kurt Ritter's vision to be the fastest growing upscale hotel company in Europe. He was later the head of the Steigenberger Hotel chain and is currently the CEO of the prestigious IHCL – the Taj Group of Hotels, where he and his team have achieved remarkable growth and financial results.

Also notable among my team was **Sanjeev Kapoor**, who worked as a young chef in various hotels with me including Varanasi and the Ashok Hotel. The company recognized his talent very early in his career and we recommended his name for opening and operating an Indian cuisine restaurant in New Zealand, which ITDC had signed as a joint venture with a local partner. He excelled in his work there, so much so that our joint venture partner never wanted him to leave. However, Sanjeev had greater vision for himself and moved up the corporate ladder at ITDC as well as HCI and quickly became a well-known celebrity chef. He has even earned a Padma Shri award for his contribution towards the promotion of Indian cuisine.

Anuraag Bhatnagar, Chief Executive Officer of The Leela Palaces, Hotels and Resorts , worked with me as the coffee shop manager at Ashok. I saw the ability and the potential in him and mentored him for the Hyderabad House. I identified him to serve the Honourable Prime Minister and other dignitaries. With his talent,intellect and hard work he has grown in the industry and today heads one of the best luxury chains in world.

Raj Rana became my executive assistant when I was head of the hotels division. When Radisson was opening a hotel in Moscow, I recommended him for a management position in the front office there. After working in Moscow for a few years he moved to the US with Radisson, became general manager and later headed the company's operations in North America till I was instrumental in selecting him to be my successor as the CEO of Carlson Hotels South Asia, which he headed for a few years. He is currently the CEO of Citymax Hotels and Foodmark, UAE (part of the Landmark Group).

Deepak Ohri, who heads the Lebua Group of Hotels in Thailand and lectures at Harvard Business School, has also been my executive assistant. **Rajesh Bharadwaj** is another member of the versatile and talented team, and is currently owner and developer of the highly acclaimed Junoon, a Michelin-star restaurant in New York City.

Chef Vinod worked with me in Varanasi and later at the Ashok Hotel, and now along with his partner Sarfaraz runs the very famous and successful Indique, which is a Michelin-star restaurant in the Washington DC area. I was only able to manifest a never-give-up philosophy thanks to the work done by **S.B. Sabharwal**, **Sanjay Mukherjee**, **Vijay Gupta**, **Balraj Bhasin**, **Cecil Samual**, **B.P. Singh, N.K. Piplani**, **Rajiv Makin**, **Sanjay Chadda**, **M.S. Gupta**, **R.C. Gulati**, **Sudhir Sibbal, Sandip Tandon** and all my executive assistants – which included Prasoon Mukherje, Raj Rana, Amitabha Bose, Kiran Prakash and Deepak Ohri. I apologize if I have missed out on some names, but I recognize it has been a collaborative effort from one and all that has executed the sails of success.

I was also lucky to have had a great initial team that helped to develop and position the Radisson Hotel Group in South Asia. These include **M.L. Bhattacharya**, **Sanjiv Tyagi**, **Pankaj Kodesia**, **Rajan Narula**, **Rupinder Garg**, **Sanjeev Pahwa**, **Saurabh Sharma**, **Nilesh Mitra, Vinita Panwar** and **Neelam Kachru**. They all deserve acknowledgment.

I have always been very particular in how I nurture my team. For me, nurturing is a process that needs a structure about it and cannot be defined by just hand-holding. Even as deadlines were a key feature of self-accountability in our plans, I recognized that the human elements involved were also important and so I made every sincere effort to get to know my mentees better both at work and outside of it. I also realized that without authentic empowerment and a lack of due support, people will hardly be motivated enough to translate their leader's or company's dream into reality. So, to create a sense of belonging, I believed in sharing our problems – mine with them, and theirs with me. Along the way I also believed that I shouldn't, at any stage, be seen as encouraging plum postings or giving opportunities only to those perceived to be my favourites, which further helped me gain respect.

I am so proud that all these people whom I interacted with at some time or the other are now stars in their own fields. Of course, my subordinates offered a serious commitment to their job, followed by loyalty and talent. Sometimes it was a challenge, but I always wanted to have team members I could trust. Some of the bonds that I made during my youth are so strong even to date, and I'm lucky to count many as my dear friends.

VIII

Ideas on Leadership

Taking a step back, but always moving forward

It has been the honour of my life to have led a team that built an edifice for Carlson Hotels and RHG in South Asia. We built this brick by brick, with not many financial resources at the start but with a great, irreplaceable commitment. In the year 2012, when I was executive vice president, South Asia, for the Carlson Rezidor Hotel Group, and we had close to 100 hotels operating, signed and in the pipeline under its glorious banner, I decided it was time to take a step back from day-to-day operations and informed the Carlson Group of my decision. I was prompted to take this decision since we had a wide and successful network of hotels under operation across India, and I had started to lose the desire to be away from home all week. It isn't that I wanted to put my boots up and retire altogether. But at this point I felt that I owed more time to myself as well as my family. I was also confident they would recognize that I could still be effective in the growth and strategic decisions of the company. They not only agreed but asked me to draft my own contract, and I was touched when they asked me to continue being Carlson's face in the region. I was also reminded that I was among very few people in the continent to have been honoured with a **Carlson fellowship**, and my complete departure was discouraged. I was redesignated as chairman, Carlson Hotels South Asia, and was asked to search for a CEO for South Asia.

In keeping with my outlook, I wanted to promote someone from within our organization but no one working in India had the required franchising or operational exposure. Meanwhile, we promoted Ronnie Lobo, who was GM and VP of our flagship hotel, to the head of operations for RHW Management Services. Along with M.L. Bhattacharya, who headed technical services, I personally looked after the core development aspects of the company. Then on a trip to Minneapolis in the summer to visit my son, I met with Raj Rana over lunch. At that time Raj was vice president of Radisson Hotels North America and was looking after operations as well as franchising. Raj had been my executive assistant during his ITDC days in the late eighties and so was already well known to me. Over the years Raj had kept in touch with me and made an effort to meet with me every time I was in Minneapolis or on his visits to Delhi. I had known Raj to be diligent and organized, and then learned he also had the requisite experience and exposure of managing franchised operations. I asked him if he would be willing to relocate to India in an elevated position as CEO of Carlson Hotels South Asia. He replied that he was just as keen to be in Delhi as it would give him an opportunity to connect with his aged mother and family here. I was elated. The company agreed with my selection and in 2013, Raj moved to India. To ensure that we had the smoothest possible transition I was asked by the company to mentor him. He and I worked as a team for two years. In the first few months, I took it upon myself to introduce him to all the owners, the industry, media, etc., for which we even travelled together to many parts of India. He was already familiar with Carlson Hotels' specifications and systems and gradually he became ready to take over.

My term as chairman was completed in three years. I had worked closely with the Radisson Hotel Group for two-and-a-half decades, and while I did get a few offers for other jobs, after so many years of our association, I could not see myself with another company. Since there cannot be two leaders doing the same job, I thought it pertinent to take a further step back and gladly accepted the position of chairman emeritus and principal advisor in 2016, which has given me the satisfaction of continuing to contribute and feeling relevant in the industry, even at my so-called pre-retirement stage.

I have loved my work and I am happy to still be working, albeit at a slightly slower pace now. This new position has given more private time with myself and my family, for which I am grateful. I also get to spend more time with friends and I am enjoying the freedom to work at my own pace after so many years. It also gave me ample time to take care of my old mother before she passed away. I get to meet my sister more frequently now. I have always led such a busy life and I'm glad to have the opportunity to enjoy the fruits of my labour with those I care for most. Watching movies and travelling frequently are just some of my indulgences. I do not have any other real hobbies as a busy work schedule throughout my life has never afforded much leisure time. I did give playing golf a try, and even trained at the Gleneagles Golf training facility in Scotland, but suffered a severe backache so I gave up the idea.

Above all, it gives me great pleasure to utilize my time to pay back the industry. I was fortunate to be elected on the executive committee of the Hotel Association of India, of which I am currently vice president. This position has given me the opportunity to serve the industry, especially during and post the pandemic, by liaising and pursuing with government authorities on matters relating to the survival and revival of our industry. I am glad that we managed to get many state governments to give tourism and hospitality an industry status, and we are now working on getting infrastructure status, which will help in overall growth by creating new destinations and increased investment. One of the major wins over the COVID-19 pandemic has been in providing ECLGS schemes, which have helped many investors and developers to manage cash-flow issues. I also devote substantial time serving on the CII's National Tourism Committee, which is an advisory role on strategy and recommendations by the industry to the government. As I've also mentioned, talent is a huge concern for our industry, and I am privileged to be nominated on the governing Board of Skill India. In this role, I am involved in launching new training initiatives.

Moving forward always involves some looking back, and at this stage of life, I can't help but dwell on ideas of effective leadership, and what remaining at the top entails. In this hospitality business, to 'stay on the top' means to remain continuously engaged, always be present, communicate effectively and maintain good relationships with one and all.

The sixth president of the United States John Quincy Adams said, 'If your actions inspire others to dream more, learn more, do more, and become more, you are a leader.' A general manager's ability to guide his staff is of the utmost importance. This person needs to be knowledgeable, efficient, cost-conscious and empathetic to run a successful organization, alongside other attributes like team development, strategic thinking and acting, innovation and following ethical business practices.

Being a good leader at a hard job is a hard job in itself. In the hospitality trade, there are certain nuances to good leadership qualities. Firstly the person must be fully dedicated to one's job; in fact, one is almost 'married' to the profession.

The secret of dealing with people is the foremost secret of success

At an impressionable age, I learned not to lose sight of human relationships at all levels.

In administration, I have always believed it is better 'to take the bull by the horns'. Often, I have chosen discussion to sort out differences, which in my experience have generally been issues of miscommunication, misunderstandings or unaligned opinions. I have given ample time to others to think and review their own thoughts and actions. I have also believed in leading with humility, and whenever I felt things were getting sour, even if seemingly, I made an extra effort to amend the situation. I realized that at such times giving people periods to cool off tremendously helps relationships. Time is in fact a definite healer and most often, things tend to iron out on their own. I have never subscribed to deliberately causing hurt to anybody or connived to win a battle, as it only makes one win enemies and not friends or well-wishers.

In as far as employees are concerned, I have believed everyone has a right to grow, and it is only healthy and normal for them to want to do so. I have encouraged internal candidates to be promoted wherever possible rather than hiring from the outside. Building bonhomie among team members is a key management responsibility. As a chief executive, I have tried to build a corporate culture that promotes teamwork and satisfaction in the workplace. To create a sense of belonging at Carlson Hotels South Asia, we organized several activities such as cricket tournaments and other competitions. At these events, employees got time to interact with corporate staff and executives, and spending just a few days together led to friendships and sharing of information and resources. Despite being led by different ownerships, our hotels supported each other pro bono in training each other's staff, especially in the F&B and IT departments.

The importance of relationships in hospitality extends far beyond one's own team. Someone once said to me, 'Franchising is like a marriage. It is in one's own hands to make the relationship work. All marriages occasionally need compromise and so do business partners.' I followed this philosophy through and through in my career. Partners who spend multiple crores to build their properties and then hand them over to our brands to manage and operate them profitably have always been given the respect due to them as they do have the right to expect us to deliver on their expectations. This has been the secret of my personal as well as the company's success. In Asia, unlike the West, ownerships expect more hand-holding from franchisors.

In hospitality, presence equals empathy for employees and results in a memorable experience for guests

In our trade, it is important for a leader to be more present and to give more while encouraging people, listening to them and allowing enough freedom to one's employees to perform. A fully engaged, empowered and happy employee will give the best results and send back satisfied guests.

True presence is more than an act of physicality. One needs to watch, listen, internalize, and act in a timely fashion. It is only when a leader empathizes with the staff and colleagues that they feel secure and happy to perform. It further allows one to build and develop relationships, which in-turn helps the leader deliver better results. Criticism without true empathy demotivates people and affects their productivity.

At a very early age, I learned that one's personality is as important as one's commitment. A nurtured personality increases one's self-esteem and lends one confidence. It reflects in a person's behaviour and attitude and includes knowing how to dress appropriately and being well groomed in one's speech, social graces and also interpersonal skills. My training and experience taught me some basic lessons, such as being present both physically and emotionally. But only showing up isn't sufficient as there is no point in just hanging around with vacant eyes or being preoccupied with one's own problems. What matters is the ability to connect with people and inspire others. I was lucky to experience such vibes from certain leaders during my tenure at ITDC, Carlson Companies and the Radisson Hotel Group. These select people come into our lives only occasionally but leave an impression that lasts a lifetime. Such people tend to carry themselves forth with poise and self-assuredness, are great visionaries, and are often ahead of their times; one can feel the shift in the air when they walk into a room. Yasser Arafat was one such personality, whom I met a few times during my tenure at the Ashok Hotel. It is his charismatic demeanour that won him the Nobel Prize in 1994 for his efforts to create peace in the Middle East.

Often the secret of strong personalities lies in the fact that they care a lot about the people they work with and the work that the team undertakes. They are strongly connected to their intuition as they move with ease through many situations in life. They demonstrate graciousness, a magnanimous compassion for others, and an ability to be flexible in a variety of circumstances and environments. People who possess a charismatic presence have a deep awareness of themselves, of others, and of what is happening around them. It is people with such traits who remain at the top.

No matter how different people seem, they all secretly want to be seen and heard

It is people who are the key to one's own success and to the success of the organization. There is an art to cultivating relationships, and once one gets the hang of it, it is easier to soar to the top of one's area of expertise. The trick to cracking the secret of developing relationships lies in a nuanced craft related to human behaviour and personality.

As a hotelier and manager, I am the first to acknowledge that yes… everyone is unique. But after years of dealing and interacting with people, I've also come to the realization that there is one thing that connects everyone – all people desire to be seen and heard, and this desire is directly connected to our fundamental uniqueness of being.

In a study about conflict resolution, it was discovered that 'being heard' plays a critical role in changes in attitudes. Even if people come from diverse cultures with complicated cultural and historical gulfs between them, they can resolve conflicts with active listening and talking. The same philosophy works in our trade when dealing with people. Everything becomes achievable through skilful conversation. Eighty per cent of our problems, both in a professional sense and daily life, especially in India, are people problems. So if we can unlock the secrets of solving these, productivity will be boosted by that much. In the hospitality business and in any other part of our lives, the better you actively listen to your guests or clients and staff, the better you will be able to serve them. An article published in the *Harvard Business Review* titled 'The Power of Listening in Helping People Change' states: 'Listening resembles a muscle.

It requires training, persistence, effort, and most importantly, the intention to become a good listener. It requires clearing one's thoughts and listening carefully – and if this isn't possible, postponing a conversation to when you can truly listen without being distracted.'

Listening carefully and offering quality feedback helps people to feel heard and understood, which also nurtures mutual respect. Basic courtesies such as limiting distractions, refraining from interruption, controlling the urge to judge, not imposing your solutions, asking more good questions and reflecting are all traits of active listening, which I have practised through my career.

Communication is the foundation of relationships

No individual can claim to achieve success without working as a team. Communication is the one activity that brings people together. It is an important management function that helps to bridge the gap between people through the flow of information and understanding between them. It is the foundation of decision-making and planning for the overall smooth and efficient working as well as facilitating coordination, increasing efficiency and promoting cooperation.

Communicating well isn't just talking well. Surprisingly, effective leadership can depend on a simple thing like listening first and speaking second. Communicating with junior employees can involve listening to their grievances and even expressing concern for their welfare, which can go a long way in earning their loyalty. I had the good fortune of having very good relationships with my employees because I always heard their point of view. I will make a special mention of the union leaders, some of whom are still in contact with me. They call me time and again even though I left my previous organization over three decades ago.

Hospitality is a people's business and is also known as a service industry. It is good communication that provides clarity and direction to employees. It is a must to be open to talk about challenges, successes and daily tasks, not only with colleagues but with all team members. They remain better informed and more engaged, which results in increased productivity and builds teamwork. Moreover, good communication skills also help enhance a guest's experience, leading to customer loyalty and increased business and eventually the hotel's success. Even in this age of electronic communication, well-executed verbal and non-verbal communication skills in the hospitality industry still hold great importance.

When in doubt, always show compassion

Compassion isn't just about feeling empathetic but more importantly acting on such an intention. If someone is struggling with a task or a challenging situation, simply feeling bad for them doesn't help them in any way. No one wants to be pitied. Action is more necessary to be truly compassionate. If you see a problem, don't just discuss it. Try to be part of the solution. And if the problem is beyond your ability, don't shy away from seeking someone's help who can tackle and solve it.

Taking interest in one's colleagues and sometimes also of one's subordinates goes a long way in building relationships. There are less chances that one would know the likes and dislikes or spouses' names of the people one works with. I have believed it is important to make an effort to learn what people like, know if they have kids or how old they are or which schools they attend. Make notes, if need be, and be genuinely interested in the person. I didn't allow myself to succumb to ego and went out of my way to look after people who weren't even necessarily in agreement with my management style. I can say with confidence that my positive behaviour with them also converted their thoughts. These people are my friends and well-wishers to date. In my life, such instances have come on and off, but I believed in being fair and took on challenges while ignoring other people's prejudices, and things sorted themselves out.

A cliché is a cliché for a reason: Change is the only constant

In my career with the Radisson Group, my focus was on franchising and managing other people's properties. In this business, both the franchisor and franchisee need to be flexible and be ready to change with the times. Those who don't change get left behind. It is important to update everything, be it the hotel decor, music, food and beverage offerings and most importantly, one's own thought process. It is this sort of flexibility that enabled us to grow our brands to such an extent. No two people are the same nor are hotel sites, so we never adopted a cookie-cutter approach towards building them. Even the food and beverage options at hotels vary, depending on what the location and market demands. At the Radisson Group, the ownership of our franchised hotels has always been fully involved from the building stage of the hotel. They have the option of choosing the architects and interior designers for their properties, either from a list of consultants who are pre-approved by the company, or after obtaining approval so long as the brand's specifications and creativity are acceptable and commensurate to our own standards.

Innovation is a cornerstone of change. No one can be a master of all trades. A good leader must allow his subordinates and partners to innovate and be open to new ideas and discussions. Giving others the freedom to develop their ideas is imperative otherwise people will lack determination and will fear taking any new initiatives.

A return on investment is more important than a return on ego

Reversing this adage, of when people prioritize a return on their ego over a return on investment, can create huge problems. Sometimes we come across hotel investors who want to develop the best product in the city, which is especially true in tier-2 and tier-3 cities. Sometimes, with such enthusiasm, they over-invest in the interiors of the property and create more facilities than required for example, night clubs or huge wellness centres and multiple restaurants. They then expect the brand to drive a rate commensurate with their investment. In such cases, there is very little chance that the return on their investment will meet their expectations; it will only be a return on their ego.

Training is useful but it is no substitute for experience

The ongoing training of employees in skill, sales and management techniques is imperative to the operation of any hotel. Getting well trained staff has always been a challenge and continues to be difficult. Each hotel tends to have its own training department, which regularly imparts and updates staff skills on the job to enable them to provide a fantastic experience to their guests. Even if trained staff is available, a hotel still needs to train them to their individual requirements. Courteous, hospitable and helpful staff will always send back happy guests.

It is important to consider that a person's softer life skills are usually honed through experience. While personality and high standards of integrity are innate orientations, but they can also be developed over time. A well-groomed, neatly turned-out employee makes the required impression on a guest. Moreover, one's actions must always be ethical and capable of winning other people's respect in the long run. My own mantra has been to 'under promise and over deliver', which is something I learned along the way, in spite of an enthusiasm to constantly perform and perform well at work, which is particularly the hallmark of young people eager to prove themselves. One must remember that actions must always be in the interest of the organization over personal gains.

An empowered team is a motivated team

A good leader will never take away the credit for good work done by a colleague. Such a move will hamper an employee's commitment, and they will lose faith in the company. They will likely stop sharing their ideas in the future. Teamwork above all leads to success. An occasional casual evening spent with one's team goes a long way in achieving a sense of belonging. I was mindful about following up with everyone on my team, because I believed they needed to be empowered to take efficient action and make decisions when necessary. When the team is empowered, they will shine in their jobs and contribute to their utmost potential. Again, empathy plays a key role in identifying that at all levels, people nurture self-actualization. In her book titled *Leading the Workforce of the Future*, thought leader Brigette Hyacinth has explained successful leadership as influence, and not authority. It is my experience that when given a chance to do more, people almost always rise to the occasion.

Sometimes leading from the front is the best course of action

Working at a hotel means frequent high-pressure situations that require active problem-solving, or firefighting, sometimes literally. In 1983, I remember a regular working day at the Ashok. I came up to my suite on the sixth floor for a lunch break, and while my meal was being set up, I went out onto the balcony for a breath of fresh air. In the distance, chaos was unfolding. Plumes of thick, grey smoke were billowing out of the hotel's gas bank, an outhouse connected to the building that housed many hundreds of interconnected cylinders. It was on fire. If the gas bank itself caught fire, it would be an unmitigated disaster not only for the hotel and its occupants but also to its surrounding areas. At that time, there were over seven to eight hundred guests and staff members at the hotel. As I rushed out of my suite into the corridor, I saw some staff members flailing about, worry etched on their faces and gait. They were looking around for help, yet no one dared go near the fire and attempt to douse it. I remember thinking: if someone didn't do something immediately, there would be a serious tragedy. There was no time to waste. I ran down the stairs, two at a time, and made my way to the ground floor and towards the gas bank. The smoke had grown thicker. I tied a handkerchief around my face to act as a rudimentary mask and managed to slip into the gas bank from a side entry. The details are sketchy now, but in that chaos I had just one goal: to stop the fire at all costs, and so I did everything in my power to douse it. From forming a basic manpower firefighting team on the spot, to delegating folks to bring in the fire extinguishers, to personally extinguishing the fire with my team's help, even today, I don't know how I found the courage to go into that smoke-filled room, but the thought of what could happen kept me going. Watching me pick up the extinguisher and enter the gas bank, the staff joined too. We collectively managed to extinguish the fire, save many lives and the property too.

After looking back, I'd also like to look forward and share some tips on pursuing a career in hospitality, borne of my experience. Like most professional fields, a degree is advisable. Institutions like Les Roches, Schweizerische Hotelfachschule, Ecole Hôtelière de Lausanne, and the Glion Institute of Higher Education in Switzerland, and the University of Nevada and Cornell University in the US are renowned for their hospitality management programmes. Closer to home, in India, the Indian School of Hospitality in Gurgaon has tied up with Les Roches, while the Pusa Institute and National Council for Hotel Management and Catering Technology still rank among the best in the country. Aside from a fundamental degree in hospitality and tourism, an MBA can go a long way in ensuring growth in the industry.

When I joined IHM Pusa, few were aware of the usefulness of advanced studies in the hospitality business and were content with completing just an undergraduate programme. Back then the industry hardly gave a post-graduate degree weightage either. However, things are different now and everyone who looks at pursuing a career in hospitality needs to have adequate knowledge of all spheres of the business. Skill training is necessary at the entry level but it is finally business acumen that will take one to higher positions. I realized this during my training period in West Germany, where I opted to be an executive assistant to the general manager rather than just focus on operations. Even after stepping into managerial positions, I focused on personal development and attended various advanced management programmes at the Indian Institute of Public Administration, Management Development Institute, Cornell University, etc.

In all, the hospitality industry is an umbrella term for a collection of business sectors that have a lot in common with each other and they work closely together. The industry itself encompasses a broad category of fields within service, which include hotels and other lodgings, food and beverage venues like bars and restaurants, event planning, theme parks, travel and tourism agencies and even hospitals. Cruise lines, retail stores and banks also tend to hire hotel management graduates, given the service nature of their operations. Such a sustained demand has resulted in long-term job opportunities, which await those interested in pursuing this promising path, especially as businesses struggle to seek and secure quality staff with the right competencies and adequate qualifications and skill sets.

According to the 2022 World Travel & Tourism Council (WTTC) Report, travel and tourism – in its direct, indirect and induced impacts – accounted for one in four of all new jobs created across the world, translating to 10.6 per cent of all jobs (334 million) and 10.4 per cent of global GDP (USD 9.2 trillion) prior to the pandemic. Meanwhile, international visitor spending amounted to USD 1.7 trillion in 2019 (6.8 per cent of total exports, 27.4 per cent of global services exports). Unfortunately, the travel and tourism sectors suffered a loss of almost USD 4.5 trillion in 2020, with the contribution to GDP dropping by a staggering 49.1 per cent as compared to 2019, relative to a 3.7 per cent GDP decline of the global economy in 2020. In 2019, the travel and tourism sectors contributed 10.4 per cent to global GDP; a share which decreased to 5.5 per cent in 2020 due to ongoing restrictions on mobility. In 2020, 62 million jobs were lost, representing a drop of 18.5 per cent, leaving just 272 million employed across the sector globally, compared to 334 million in 2019. While the threat of job losses persists in current climatic and political conditions, many withheld jobs are currently supported by government retention schemes and reduced hours. In India, the current growth trend in the hospitality sector is now gaining stead. The middle class are travelling again – and even more than ever before, perhaps due to a pent-up demand for travel during the recent lockdowns, leading to a substantial increase of hotel tariffs and air travel.

In this vein, nearly all markets will continue to witness a year-on-year growth in near future. Certain cities saw the RevPar (or revenue per available room) growth of 100 per cent in the 1st quarter of 2023. Over the next two years, I believe we will see a higher demand and rise in rates in metropolitan towns and all leisure destinations, and since lack of scale remains a serious problem especially in tier-2 and tier-3 towns – which I consider real growth potential markets, with an average size of hotels with fifty to eighty rooms or less – an insufficient supply may result in higher rates all around. Moreover, with a focus on creating new travel destinations along with airport enhancement, including the government's expectation to have 220 operating airports in the country by 2026, infrastructure development will be greatly enhanced and create many job opportunities in the sector going forward. I pin my hopes on an authentic and effective '**Incredible India**' and Tourism promotion on mission mode campaign to attract more institutional investors as well.

IX

Flashbacks and Memorable Experiences

Make plans, but life happens

The beauty of life exists in this duality: the most well-laid plans can be our guide, while the deviations from those plans can be our lessons. For me, my most memorable experiences are simply those that have left indelible memories, some sad but mostly good. From early childhood reminisces of visiting restaurants with my father, to professional opportunities whose long-lasting benefits I still enjoy today, the journey has been deep and vast, sometimes peppered with unique personal encounters that sound unbelievable, if they were not true.

Surviving an Earthquake

A 7.2 magnitude earthquake occurred in Cebu, Philippines, in October 2013. Many of us from the Radisson team had collected there at one of our properties for the annual business conference for the Asia-Pacific region. The conference was well attended not only by corporate officials but also the owners, partners and general managers of most of our franchised and managed properties. To my great delight, at a gala I was bestowed with the prestigious President's Award from Simon Barlow, president, Carlson Asia-Pacific who openly valued my contributions towards the growth of the company in Asia. Simon has been one of the most dynamic presidents and we got along well both at professional and personal level.

The earthquake first hit shortly after 8 a.m. the next morning. Neelam and I were still lying in bed when the hanging lights near the curtain began rocking from side to side. Soon we could hear the tiles in the bathrooms clang and clatter as they fell upon the glass doors of the shower cubicle. Huddled in our room on the seventeenth floor, where the floor beneath our feet had seemed to disappear, Neelam and I took refuge under the comforter simply waiting for the ceiling to fall on us. Even as death felt imminent, all of a sudden the shaking became less pronounced and a deafening silence began to encroach on us. In this moment we found both courage and disbelief, as if we had been given a second life. We aimed to make our way downstairs as soon as possible, but first eased ourselves in what remained of the broken toilet, changed into presentable clothes, packed our passports, money and some personal items in a carry-on bag. Downstairs other conference attendees shared stories about how their food had just fallen off the tables and trays. There was great pandemonium as everyone gathered in the open lawns by the swimming pool, dreading news of a potential tsunami warning as we were just 500 metres from the sea. To our relief it was only at noon that we learned we had been spared.

Two hundred people died that day in Cebu and several thousands were injured. We had been lucky as there were no casualties at our hotel, just minor injuries. The company arranged special flights to evacuate some of our partners and owners from Cebu the same day. Vice president and general manager Lyle Lewis and his team did a commendable job of taking care of each and every guest with warmth and care, as they continued to be on duty in spite of the circumstances. Intense earthquake aftershocks continued for the next twenty-four hours. Some were so massive that we had to run out of the building when the earth shook. Fortunately the building didn't suffer severe damage and that is why we are still alive. Having said that, even the granite cladding in the lobby had fallen, but luckily no one was seriously hurt. Most didn't dare to sit or sleep in the lobby and slept out on the lawns instead. Somehow we felt more comfortable inside and slept on the sofas in the lobby that night. With the help of some very courageous staff, we managed to retrieve our baggage from our room the next day. As we waited in the airport lounge the next afternoon, there was another major aftershock. We were afraid if the runway got damaged, we wouldn't be able to take off. It is only when we were airborne that we heaved a sigh of relief. We donated whatever local currency we had and decided never to return there again.

A Hijacking Saga

On 10 September 1976, my wife and our one-and-half-year-old son boarded an Indian Airlines flight from Delhi to Aurangabad, which was a hopping flight via Jaipur and Udaipur. Previously, Neelam and I had travelled to Delhi together and were seated next to Mr Avtar Singh, a regular customer of the Aurangabad Ashok Hotel, who had become a friend too. Since he was much older than us, we started calling him 'uncle'. He and Neelam got into a conversation about travel and decided they would take a trip together to Pakistan. I was concerned about the visa hassles so I didn't consent to the trip, but sometimes we do ordain things upon ourselves. Neelam took a last-minute decision to fly on this particular return flight to Aurangabad, along with our son, to surprise me as I had already returned. She had run into Uncle at the airport and they checked-in together. Mr Deshpande, the chief engineer at ITDC, was also on the flight. Meanwhile, in Aurangabad, I left for the airport to receive the chief engineer, but the airport manager informed me that the flight had gone missing. I was aggrieved for Mr Deshpande's family and returned to the hotel. Soon after I received a telex from the airport manager saying that Neelam and Amit were also on board. I cannot describe the confusion and fear that I felt. I locked myself in my office trying to prepare myself for the worst as in most cases, especially in those days, when planes went missing, they most often crashed. But then I received word that the plane had landed in Lahore and was immediately flooded with relief knowing that my family was alive.

But all was still not well. The flight had been hijacked. Neelam had taken Amit to the washroom when the hijackers first made themselves known, so she had no idea what kind of situation was underway. On her return to her seat, she requested one of the men blocking the isle to move. She requested him several times in English, and then thought maybe the person didn't understand the language so she tried to make her way by tapping his shoulder. Mr Deshpande yelled at her to quickly return to her seat, as it was one of the highjackers whose shoulder she had tapped, and he had a grenade in his hand. There were five hijackers on board, each armed with grenades or country-made pistols, threatening to blow up the plane if passengers didn't cooperate. Soon all of the passengers saw the commander pilot being escorted to the rear bathroom at gunpoint. The hijackers went around taking down the names of each passenger, ascertaining the VIPs on board, and the passengers cautioned each other to not disclose who they were and furnish their names instead. When the aircraft started to descend, the hijackers ordered everyone to put their hands up in the air, reprimanding or threatening anyone who gave way to fatigue.

Amit, our son, was still on formula milk and Neelam needed to constitute it with hot water in order to feed him. On her request, one of the hijackers escorted her to the galley and they both got into a conversation. Neelam had heard them conversing with one another and knew that they were Kashmiri. She understood Kashmiri and asked him where they were from. He didn't believe that she was Kashmiri, so she told him that she was married to one and understood the language well. He spoke fluent Urdu and was inquisitive enough to find out where I hailed from but didn't divulge his own origins. Neelam was brave. She then urged them to serve breakfast with the aid of the air hostesses, and even specially requested they get a tandoori chicken lunch from the Pakistan Airport authorities. Intending to commandeer the flight to Jeddah, the hijackers made demands on the airport authorities who delayed refuelling in order to buy time. As the day progressed, the toilets became dirty and since Amit was still being toilet-trained, she unexpectedly asked one of the hijackers to take him down to the tarmac to relieve himself, knowing that the Pakistani security forces would never allow him to run away with her baby. Towards the afternoon, the hijackers allowed some passengers to leave as they were delirious. They offered Neelam a chance to leave with Amit too, but she refused.

Eventually the hijackers grew more lenient and even allowed the passengers to move around the cabin. Amit was blissfully unaware of the situation and happily moved around offering others the solace of innocence. Around midnight, the ladies were allowed to deplane. There was a tourist group from Germany and the women refused to deplane without their male partners. Neelam, who spoke German, convinced them that it was only after the women left that the men would be released too. They spent the night in the transit lounges at the airport, and the next day, when the airport had re-opened to regular traffic, another Indian Airlines plane was sent to Lahore to bring the passengers back to Delhi.

The only status updates available were what the *Doordarshan* and other media put out, which was very limited. I was glued to the Press Trust of India (PTI) news printer at the hotel, in the hope of any information on their release. With God's grace, they returned to Delhi the next evening. The press hounded Neelam for some time for the inside story. Amit and her photograph was plastered on the front page of all the major dailies. Allegedly the hijackers were demanding the release of some of their comrades who were locked in Indian jails. One of the key questions they probed her on was why she didn't opt to deplane with the other women. The truth was that she felt she was inappropriately dressed and also had no money or passport on her. In hindsight, it was a thoughtful decision as those who had deplaned in the afternoon had had a traumatic time returning home via the Wagah Border in Punjab.

Waylaid in Europe

Among holidays with family and friends, road trips are always particularly special. We had been wanting to take such a trip with our friends Pradeep and Neelam Anand since the early nineties, and finally our dream came true in 2017. We began our trip in Nice from where we drove to Cannes to stay at a friend's holiday home. From there, we drove to Florence and onwards to Rome. On our way to Rome, we had two experiences which remain etched in our memories. First we decided to take the scenic route. After the first half hour, paved roads gave way not only to hilly terrain but also a dirt track, which was not metalled. The incline uphill suddenly became very steep and because the road was muddy, we started to skid back. There was also no other vehicle along our route and we feared we would lose control of the situation, especially being in a foreign country. We steadied ourselves and navigated our way through the path and arrived at a plateau that offered a breath-taking view of the vineyards. Our earlier fright quickly gave way to awe.

Later, we stopped at a fashion outlet mall and piled our loot into the boot of our rented Mercedes SUV. We were only a few miles short of Rome and were jubilantly discussing the success of our journey when a car drove up to us on the highway. Two men drew our attention by flashing police badges and asking up to stop. Thinking we may have been speeding, we pulled up to the kerb. The police car parked their vehicle just in front of ours. An officer approached the car and announced he was from the narcotics department and asked to check our bags. One by one, he checked our handbags and the ladies' purses. Then he asked for our passports, which we obediently handed over to him. Next he said that we would need to follow them to the police station. At this point we rebelled – since we were innocent, we refused to go to the police station. My wife Neelam's instinct intimated to her that they were frauds. She kept saying to note their car number, but we were all so disoriented we couldn't bring ourselves to memorize it. Neelam opened her door and stepped onto the highway. She began to ask cars to stop for help, but no help was forthcoming. She got back into the car and said in Hindi, '*Yeh chor hain*!' (They are thieves!) To this the man promptly replied, 'No *chor*!' Now we were all convinced that we were in the process of being waylaid. Neelam suddenly took notice of the man's jacket, which had the Champion brand logo on it. When she pointed that out to me, I quickly got out of the door to apprehend the man. He realized that we had understood that they were frauds, so he threw our passports inside our car and ran to their vehicle ahead of us. God was with us and we were saved from a disastrous outcome. We realized later that there was an exit a few minutes away and had we listened to them, they could've left us with no cash, credit cards, passports and perhaps have taken the car too, which had a French registration. We had forgotten that we were in Italy and that too in Rome, where people have had similar experiences driving on highways.

A few years before this incident, I had taken a cruise on the Mediterranean with my whole family. Before arrival at any port, the ship runs highlights on their TV channel for the next day's port of call. They show the sight-seeing spots and announce the do's and don'ts at the destination. Since we were docking in Naples, they warned us of how swindlers frauded tourists in the city. Once we docked in Naples, we visited Capri. After a most memorable trip to the beautiful island of Capri, we stopped to see the wares that the wayside vendors had just outside the port. One Italian vendor in a typical black suit got after our son Amit to buy a laptop at a throwaway price. His wife Bhavna needed a new laptop so he went for it. Each one of us scrutinized the laptop properly to see if it worked alright. When all of us were convinced, Amit paid the guy and was handed over the laptop bag, as we all looked on. Another Indian vendor, who was selling leather goods, tried to hint to us not to buy it from him but we realized this in retrospect. When we crossed the road towards the entrance of the port, Amit realized we'd been had. The bag's zip just wouldn't open. When we put the bag on the belt for the security screening, the port staff began to feel sorry for us. There were only packets of salt in the bag and no laptop. When and how the person had exchanged the bags still remains a mystery.

Drowning in Goa

In 1995, after we returned to India from Singapore, my colleague Jim Olson and his wife Jacque visited India. We accompanied them on a short trip to Goa, where we stayed at the Leela Hotel. Soon after checking in, Neelam and I decided to make use of our free time and quickly rushed to the beach. The water was only about knee-deep and the sea was very inviting, so we waded into the sea around 100 metres from the shore. With every passing minute the size of the waves grew and along with a group of foreigners we enjoyed riding them. I told Neelam that I wanted to exercise a bit and began to swim back, while she preferred to enjoy the water for a while longer.

Suddenly the waves got so big that I had difficulty in swimming back to the shore. On finally reaching I realized no one else was swimming in the sea except for my wife. I tried to gesture to her to swim back but soon realized that she was being taken further into the sea with each undulation. Due to fear her energy was depleting but fortunately sense prevailed and she decided to just stay afloat and not expend her remaining energy in trying to swim back to the shore. She later told me that she felt by that time there was about 20 feet of water below her. At this stage, standing all alone on the beach, I had two choices: one was to try to save her and the other was to save my own self from drowning along with her. I chose the latter as I was sure I couldn't swim well enough to reach her, leave alone bring her back with me. Wondering what our children, who were studying overseas, would have done if we had both drowned kept me helplessly transfixed at her struggle in the deep water. Out of nowhere, two dark complexioned men emerged from the sea. I told them to save Neelam but it took them a few minutes to spot her head, the only part of her body that was visible when the waves receded. They swam towards her and brought her back and threw her in my arms. Before we could both turn around and profusely thank them, they were gone, not to be seen anywhere. With tears in my eyes I confessed to Neelam I actually watched her struggling for life and took a conscious decision to save myself from drowning with her for the sake of our children. I believe to date there was some divine intervention and perhaps even the result of some good karma that she survived.

Performing Predictions

In the mid 1980s when I was the officer on special duty to the managing director of ITDC, we were asked to interview some astrologers to employ one at the Ashok Hotel. For the longest time the Ashok had had an astrologer who had made predictions for the guests and a lot of them had come true. Guests would frequently choose to stay at the hotel so that they could have their futures predicted. He was a freelancer and charged the guests directly. When he left, guests would still ask for an astrologer so we advertised for the position. The interview was held in my office. When interviewing a particular candidate, I was at a loss of what questions to ask, so I asked the candidate to tell me something about our past and predict the future. One candidate, named Partho Bhattacharya, first told me snippets from my past, which were reasonably accurate and then he said to me, 'Sir, you will not be sitting on this chair after fifteen days.' I was both amused and shocked to have someone say something so directly in an interview; it needed guts. We were impressed with his confidence and knowledge as well as the media coverage he had received. We all agreed that he was the best candidate as he knew palmistry along with astrology and thus, he was offered the job as assistant manager, astrology.

Needless to say, his prediction came out true. Within fifteen days I was transferred and promoted to senior vice president, something that I didn't really expect. I then decided to show him my horoscope and asked him to write down his predictions for me for the next ten to fifteen years. He wrote that good things were in store for me and made some unimaginable predictions – like I would leave my Government job. Since he had said good things, I didn't discuss or ponder over anything that he had indicated. Being satisfied with the overall outcome of his study of my horoscope, I put it away in my drawer in my hotel room, where we lived. I never read it again and also forgot about this paper.

In July 1991, when I resigned from my job at ITDC and was sorting out my things while packing for Singapore, I came across the paper on which Partho had predicted my future. I became curious to find out if he had predicted when I would leave my job, and on top of that, relocate to Singapore. To my utmost surprise he had predicted the year and even month correctly. He had written that I would move to a seaside country.

We moved to Singapore in July 1991 and in August I received a call from Partho telling me that he was in Singapore. For some reason I couldn't meet with him, but I gave him our home address and asked him to meet my wife. Neelam told me that he came to the house and said, 'Madam, you seem to be totally settled here, but you will not settle down here. You will have to return to India in around four years.' Neelam wasn't happy to hear that as the kids had not even started to attend their schools in Singapore. The very thought of moving back at that time didn't excite either of us. But if destiny has something pre-ordained, it is bound to happen. So, once again Partho's prediction came out true. Ever since then he and I have remained in touch. Once a year he brings a paper with fresh predictions for me. Having said this, I do not allow his predictions to steer my life. I only read the predictions carefully once the time has passed as it is wise to consider that not all predictions are 100 per cent accurate.

Another person whom we go to in our time of need is Santoshi Mataji, who has her ashram in Kankhal, Haridwar. My in-laws were her devotees and my mother-in-law in particular visited her ashram frequently. Mataji gave her lots of blessing and respect too, so much so Neelam used to tease her mother that Mataji was her best friend.

Once I decided to leave ITDC and before we left for Singapore, Neelam went to visit her parents. One evening when her mother was going to meet Mataji, Neelam said she wanted to accompany her to seek Mataji's blessings. She went with a lot of questions on her mind. We were leaving the country and what lay ahead was unknown. Would the kids settle down in their studies in a foreign atmosphere? Would I be successful in my work? After all, developing hotel brands was different to heading a hotel chain.

On arriving in Mataji's chamber she and her mother sat on a sofa, while Mataji was engaged in conversation with a gentleman who was seated on the carpet. Mataji spoke to him for about ten minutes and to Neelam's surprise all thc questions that she wanted to ask Mataji were already answered. To add to this surprise, Mataji turned towards Neelam and said, 'Have all your questions been answered or do you still have some doubts?' I do believe that saints are born with a sixth sense, and maybe they meditate so much that they do have some supernatural powers.

Santoshi Mataji also visited us in Singapore. In fact, she stayed at our house for three days. Neelam showed her the city and we felt blessed that she agreed to my mother-in-law's request for her to stay with us, enroute to the US. One day Neelam Anand, our very dear friend, came over to seek her blessings. She told her that they would be returning to India soon. She also told Neelam that we would be returning too, but not yet. This is what happened – the Anands returned in 1993 and we came back to India in 1995.

Till date, when something disturbs our peace of mind, we pick up the phone and seek her guidance and blessings. When my daughter-in-law Gazzal was going through a tough pregnancy, she told her which prayer book to read, and said that she should not worry, as she would be blessed with a healthy daughter. Lo and behold! Ashyra was born a healthy baby and her prediction that it would be a baby girl came true too.

On one of Santoshi Mataji's trips to Delhi, my son Sameer and his wife Gazzal accompanied Neelam to visit her at someone's farmhouse, where she was residing for a day. Sameer asked her if his son Aahil would play cricket. Her response was, 'Only if you take interest and invest your time in the sport.' Aahil is currently training to be a professional cricketer. Sameer remembers what Mataji had said to him. However, there are times when he cannot devote so much time to be personally present during his training and leaves it to the coaches to train him. At these times he has always had to regret and take over. Whenever he is not personally involved, even for a few days, Aahil's game gets adversely affected. Hopefully Sameer will continue to be able to take out time to be physically present going forward and we are all awaiting the day when Aahil will grow up and wear the Indian jersey.

X

Predictions on the Future

The sun rises in the present and speaks of the future

When we are born, we develop resources at an early stage on how to navigate life through learning and instinct. Life doesn't come with a training manual, so each of us must figure out how to lead our own lives. Although we are first taught by our parents and teachers, finally we learn from our own experiences. We are responsible for creating our own future and personalities. As we progress in years, those of us who don't learn how to get ahead by bettering ourselves the right way, whatever way that is, get left behind.

A body of knowledge that I have kept a close companion is that of spirituality, which to me means leading life's journey by keeping my ego in a positive state – maintaining my self-esteem and respectability, garnering belief in myself to work with dedication, and always creating an environment of love and generosity of giving, especially to the needy, deprived and the young. Spirituality reflects in compassion, gratitude, showing appreciation and returning kindness. I sincerely believe that I have received divine blessings through my life. Sharing my success with a higher power reminds me to be grateful and creates an understanding that while life is full of attachment to things, money, people, power, etc., at some stage we can lose what we are attached to.

Human nature is such that we sometimes do end up generating suffering for ourselves. We are ourselves responsible for every thought we have and deed we perform. It is therefore a choice we have, either to forget the bad events and carry on with happiness or constantly dwell on the ill-doings of others for the longest time. I have managed to consciously practice forgetting the bad and remembering the good, which to me is a state of greater illumination, because with great acceptance comes great ease. If there is a lesson for reality I'd like to impart from my own experiences, humility with agility would be it.

Those who know me – and now you do too – will know that I have always been a proponent of planning my foreseeable future in advance and then working towards achieving those objectives. With the exception of unexpectedly quitting the public sector, the act of planning has served as the pillar of support for my life and I have held fast to this mantra, whenever possible.

I wish to continue working while I am still healthy and fit enough to do so. To keep healthy I prefer not to rush through any chore and I like to prepare well in advance for everything possible. I exercise discretion in my eating habits and believe in taking small helpings; I even weigh myself twice a day and in the last forty years, I have weighed largely the same. I also make sure I take a minimum of 10,000 steps a day. My late father-in-law used to say, 'You go crazy if you retire when you are still healthy enough to work.'

I have been fortunate to have received many recognitions including the most prestigious 'Fellowship Award' from my company, as well as the larger tourism and hospitality industry throughout my career. Given their international prestige, those accolades conferred on me by global institutions are the dearest to my heart. Receiving lifetime achievement awards at ITB in Berlin, Germany; the Hotel Investment Conference – South Asia; and Hotelier India, as well as a Gallery of Legends award by India Hospitality is real acknowledgement of the efforts I had once set out with intentions so many years ago. It is a privilege that recently I was named as a torchbearer of the hotel industry by Hotelier India, along with Mr P.R.S. Oberoi. I have also received the HIFI Tourism Ratna; an Award of Excellence by the Indian Federation of Culinary Associations; a Hall of Fame Award by the Pusa Institute Hotel Management Alumni Association in 2017 – among others. While it is a great honour to receive these awards, they have more importantly served me as a challenge to continue to do better.

Though I decided to take a step back from being actively involved in operations as the company grows its portfolio of hotels all over India, I am still involved in the company's growth strategy and serve on the board of directors of all Radisson-related companies in India. I also devote a lot of time to industry-related activities and continue to serve on the boards of Skill India and the Hotel Association of India as well as advise various industry forums.

I am also on the Board of United Way Delhi, of which I am currently vice chairman. United Way is a non-profit organization affiliated with the United Way Worldwide family, which is one of the world's largest charitable organizations across forty-one countries. Their mission is to improve the lives of 'every person in every community' in a measurable and sustainable way. Some of their programmes include developing school-readiness in children, providing quality education, improving severe sanitation issues, etc. I have also personally contributed to SOS Children's Villages India to support and empower young girls. Time permitting, I would happily increase my philanthropic contributions.

With the gift of more time, I'm glad to finally have an opportunity to indulge myself, which often involves watching good television programming and keeping up with the latest movie releases. I also enjoy going out to cafés and restaurants with my friends and family, and hold travel as a dear pastime. In these moments I often think back to something the

Dalai Lama has said: 'The roots of all goodness lie in the soil of appreciation for goodness.' I interpret this statement in a few ways. First, the having of goodness begins long before the good has been had. Second, one must appreciate goodness in all its forms, including the bad. Third, like the soil is tilled by manual labour, an appreciation of goodness can be cultivated.

My older son Amit now works at a senior management position at Medtronic. He is equally dedicated to his work as he was to his studies while at the University of Minnesota – and we are both proud parents. As I shared, Amit found his life partner in Bhavna, who is also from Delhi. We try to visit them every year in the summer at their home in Minneapolis, where we look forward to spending time with our granddaughter Anya, who is also a good student like her father. Bhavna is home proud and a good cook. Meanwhile, our younger son Sameer and his wife Gazzal married in 2004 and chose to remain at home with us. Gazzal is an extremely caring person and is more a friend to us than a daughter-in-law. Sameer is innovative and entrepreneurial. He is currently involved in sports management and runs a joint venture with Mickey Arthur, the world-acclaimed, legendary cricket coach. Their son Aahil, who is now fourteen-years-old, and their daughter Ashyra, now twelve-years-old, both add years to our lives. The house is bustling with activity thanks to them.

We take a vacation almost every year, mostly in Europe with the entire family. We have enjoyed many cruise holidays with Regent Cruises, which once belonged to Carlson Companies. These holidays have been very special, being the only time when Amit, Sameer and all of us get to connect and enjoy together. It gives Neelam and me immense pleasure to see everyone laugh and eat and play together and I hope that this togetherness will continue till the end.

When I think of all the goodness in my life, what comes to mind is the people I've been blessed to share it with. From my parents, wife, children and grandchildren, to extended family, friends, colleagues and acquaintances – I've been lucky to have wonderful, or in the very least meaningful, interactions with most people I've crossed paths with or been connected to.

I want to take this opportunity to express my gratitude first to my parents, who were responsible for shaping my personality in my youth and for teaching me humility above all, which has been my greatest strength over the years, in life and at work. My life would have charted a different course without my wife, who not only tolerated my idiosyncrasies but also supported me in innumerable ways, from looking after my parents and single-handedly bringing up the children to being a stellar companion at work as well. My children and grandchildren make my life a complete pleasure with their love and caring. My friends have shouldered our relationships in inspiring ways, and have remained by my side through the thick of it.

I owe my success to the unflinching support I received from all my bosses and colleagues. No one individual can build a company or a success story. It is always teamwork, and the commitment of my teams has been imperative for the growth of our company. I could always count on my subordinates for putting in their best effort. They say it is rare to come across people who are dedicated and trustworthy. However, I can say that I have always been fortunate to have had a good team. Even those people who initially joined the flanks with a negative attitude changed their mindset and soon became engulfed in the passion we all shared for our work. Without them, I would have achieved nothing.

I also owe a special thanks to my colleagues in the over-arching hospitality industry. I am much obliged by the respect and recognition accorded to me and have felt encouraged by their validation of my efforts through media attention and lifetime achievement awards. I hope to continue to add value to the industry and look forward to the bright, youthful future that is poised to dawn in India.

Carlson / Radisson Hotels Group

Global Leadership Team of Carlson Company, 1992

South Asia Leadership Team,
Radisson Hotel Group, 2023
(Image Courtesy of Hotelier India)

Opening of First Radisson Red
at Chandigarh

Global Leadership Team of Radisson Hotel Group, 2023

Awards and Accolades

Carlson Rezidor President's Award
Philippines

Aatithya Ratna Award – HIFI

HICSA Lifetime Achievement Awardees

Hall of Fame Award
PATWA, ITB Berlin

Lifetime Achievement
Food Award

Awards and Accolades

Lifetime Achievement Award,
Hotelier India

Global Champion Award,
Radisson Hotels International

Honoured with Fellowship Award,
Minneapolis, USA

Franchise Leader of the Year,
World Franchise Congress

Honoured by World Chef's Society

Legends Award by
Tourism Minister Ms. Ambika Soni

Industry Representation

US-India Trade Agreement Forum

Uttarakhand Investors Summit

South Asian Hoteliers Conclave

Executive Committee, Hotel Association of India

Industry Representation - G20

Indonesian Tourism Minister
with Industry Colleagues

Industry Colleagues

Minister of Tourism, Govt. of Spain

The Current Secretary General of
UN-WTO and CEO of WTTC

Travel & Tourism
Industry Colleagues

Union Minister of Tourism (Govt. of India)
Chief Minister, Goa and Australian Minister

Family

Family

Family

Family

Family

Friends

Friends